THE HIGH-PERFORMING TEACHER

by
Lee Canter

A Publication of Lee Canter & Associates

Contributing Writers
Mark Falstein
Marcia Shank

Editorial Staff
Marlene Canter
Jacqui Hook
Barbara Schadlow
Kathy Winberry

Design
Carol Provisor

Cover Design
The Arcane Corporation

Photographer
Barry Slobin

©1994 Lee Canter & Associates
P.O. Box 2113, Santa Monica, CA 90407-2113
800-262-4347   310-395-3221

Printed in the United States of America
First printing March 1994
98 97 96 95   10 9 8 7 6 5 4 3 2

Library of Congress Catalog Card Number 94-94161
ISBN 0-939007-82-7

This book is dedicated to five special high-performing teachers who embody the ideas set forth in its pages.

Velvet McReynolds

Debra Peppers

Gail Schack

Joyce Schneider

Vic Schneidman

Thank you for welcoming us into your classrooms and sharing the secrets of your success.

Contents

Acknowledgements

The "High-Performing Teacher" was initially developed as a course for teachers who, while feeling loyal to the profession and sincerely needed by their students, were increasingly dispirited about the many problems they faced daily in the classroom.

The ideas, skills, techniques and inspiration for helping teachers renew their passion and joy for the art of teaching came to me from many sources. I am deeply grateful for the talent and assistance of the following practitioners in the field and writers and editors on our staff:

Craig Arnold

Mark Falstein

Jacqui Hook

Linda Manuel

Velvet McReynolds

Debra Peppers

Carol Provisor

Gail Schack

Barbara Schadlow

Joyce Schneider

Vic Schneidman

Marcia Shank

Kathy Winberry

Introduction

Twenty years ago, I was a young special education teacher with a crusading desire to work closely with children and have a positive impact on their lives. During those early years, there were times I faced challenges in the classroom I thought were unsolvable. There were times I felt students may be beyond my influence, and times I was uncertain where to turn for help.

Though it could be very frustrating, I was determined to succeed in the profession I loved. I came to school each day resolved to try something new to ignite the spark in those students whom I had difficulty reaching. I knew I just had to find the right strategies to use with these students. Lee witnessed my predicament and helped me construct an approach to classroom behavior management that worked—for me and for the kids. That's how our first program, Assertive Discipline, was born.

In fact, it was the eventual nationwide success of Assertive Discipline that unexpectedly took me out of the classroom and into the world of business. Lee and I, through our company, Lee Canter and Associates, began developing other training programs for teachers and parents in need of better ways of helping children.

Over the years we began to see that even when given the skills to succeed with the most difficult, challenging students in their classrooms, too many teachers still remained frustrated, burned out and on the verge of leaving the profession that they too loved. I was distressed to think that we may be losing some of our best teachers—

those who could be our greatest hope for having a significant influence on the youngsters who might become the leaders, movers and shakers of our society.

I thought back to some of the helpful training I received in the business world that, interestingly, brought out and renewed the passion I once felt for teaching, and how I was taught the importance of incorporating that feeling into my daily life as a businesswoman.

As Lee and I explored this issue, we began to see that we needed to offer a program that helped teachers rekindle their passion for teaching much as I did. To be able to guide their students expertly, calmly and confidently, teachers need to know exactly how to make each day the very best for each child, and the best for themselves too. If they could get back in touch with the reasons that brought them to teaching in the first place and renew their motivation and excitement, they could feel empowered to take control of their daily teaching lives.

Our goal in The High-Performing Teacher is to teach the skills that ultimately encourage teachers to continue their mission in this noblest of professions. We want to help teachers feel less frustrated and burned out so they once again feel excited and empowered in the classroom, knowing that they are shaping the future.

As Lee was writing this book, the techniques of the program were already a reality with the several thousand teachers who had participated in the High-Performing Teacher graduate course on video. Their excitement and renewed enthusiasm for teaching inspired us, and I hope after reading this book, you will also be inspired to turn your hard times in the classroom into a feeling of satisfaction and success.

We are here every day to be of assistance to you. Please write and let us know some of the challenges you are facing and what you are doing to overcome them. We invite you to share your successes with us.

On behalf of Lee and our entire company, I sincerely hope that this teaching year is your best ever.

Marlene Canter
March 1994

The Power of You

One of the most difficult, stressful occupations today must surely be that of the classroom teacher. Who else is charged with the awesome responsibility of preparing our children for the future? And who else is expected to fulfill this critical responsibility in the face of so many roadblocks?

Teaching today is a more complex, more demanding profession than it ever was in the past. Just consider some of the challenges you typically face:

- students who come to school unprepared to learn.

- students who are unmotivated and disruptive.

- students with attention-deficit disorders.

- students who are verbally or physically abusive.

- students who come to school armed with lethal weapons.

- parents who are openly hostile to your efforts.

- administrators who won't back you up.

- lack of funding, lack of books, lack of supplies.

- parents who disregard the importance of learning.

And what does society at large have to say about these challenges? All too often they blame *you,* the teacher. Hardly a week goes by that some politician, journalist or other self-appointed expert doesn't make a point of telling you how you're failing:

- "You should be motivating the students!"

- "You should be raising their self-esteem!"

- "You should be helping them reach their full potential!"

- "Whatever happened to dedicated teachers?"

- "You work six hours a day, you get three months' vacation every year, and you want *more money?*"

But let me ask, who motivates *you?* Who takes care of *your* self-esteem? Who helps you to reach *your* full potential? As I see it, the "crisis in education" isn't only about curriculum, competence or community support. It's also about too many teachers being over-whelmed by the challenges. It's about too many teachers losing the belief that they can make a difference in the lives of their students. It's about too many excellent, committed teachers burning out.

> *You can regain your belief that you can make a difference.*

But you *can* overcome the challenges. You *can* make a difference. And that's what this book is all about.

The High-Performing Teacher will show you how to empower yourself to make a difference in the classroom every day of the year.

This book will show you how to regain and maintain your confident belief that you *can* make a difference. It is a blueprint for overcoming negativity, despair and hopelessness, for truly making an impact on your students—and for enjoying yourself in the process.

In this book, you'll learn how teachers facing the same challenges you face have met and overcome them—in many cases going from near-burnout situations to an effectiveness recognized by students, parents, colleagues and administrators.

You'll learn skills that will help you become the best teacher you can possibly be.

You'll learn how to stay in touch with the potential influence you have over your students—to go home every evening feeling satisfied that you truly did make a difference in the lives of your students that day.

> *The high-performing teacher is one who knows that he or she makes a difference in students' lives.*

Teachers Can Have a Profound Impact on Students' Lives

Any teacher can become a high-performing teacher, one who has a positive impact on the lives of students. The way you do it is by *making choices,* by choosing behaviors that enable you to respond successfully to the challenges.

These behaviors are strategies that you can learn.

In fact you must learn them. The future of our nation depends on it. *You have the most important job in America today.* We cannot afford to allow you, the classroom teacher, to lose your belief in your ability to positively influence students.

Belief is critical to your success. "If you believe you can, you can. If you believe you can't, you can't." Don't dismiss this notion as a fable about a little train engine chugging up a hill. Beliefs are powerful. According to one study, eighty-five percent of our success is a function of what we *believe* to be true about our capabilities.

The belief in your power to make a difference is another strategy that you can learn.

One reason I feel so passionate about the importance of your job, about the importance of your belief in yourself, is because a teacher made a profound difference in my own life. It is no exaggeration to state that I would not be doing what I am doing today were it not for this teacher.

His name is John Nicholson, and he was my high-school English teacher. On my very first day in his class, he told us, "Through the choices you make, you shape your destiny."

Now when I entered John Nicholson's class, I was a seventeen-year-old with few goals and little direction. In fact, a counselor had recently said to me, "Lee, you don't have what it takes to even go to college"—and I believed it. *I believed I didn't "have what it takes"!*

> *Through the choices you make, you shape your destiny*

So when Mr. Nicholson started talking about choices and destiny, it didn't make much of an impact. I just rolled my eyes, like kids do. When he assigned us an essay to write, I gave it my usual half-baked effort. The paper came back, and on top of it was my grade—a very poor grade.

I thought, wait a minute. I'm no genius, but I don't get grades like *this*.

I sat down with him and he said, "Lee, you know something? You make poor choices. You have more ability than you realize. You're just not putting out the effort you're capable of." I sat there, but I was barely listening.

I rewrote the paper with minimal effort. The grade came back—more poor marks.

I don't need this, I told myself. This guy's got an attitude problem. I'm getting out of here.

I went home and told my mother, "Mom, there's this teacher who's really on my case. I want out of his class."

My mother said, "His name is Mr. Nicholson, right?"

"Yeah, how'd you know?"

"He just called and told me, 'No matter what your son says, don't let him drop this course.'"

So I went back to class, and he assigned another essay to write. The grade came back and once again it was poor.

This was too much. I told myself, "I can't do anything right for this teacher. Worse comes to worst, I'll flunk the class and make it up in summer school."

Mr. Nicholson sat me down to talk about the paper. He really analyzed it in detail. Meanwhile, I was saying, "Yeah, yeah, I know. I flunked and all that."

He said, "You know, I've had students like you before, and I bet I know what you're thinking right now. You're thinking you can flunk the course and make it up in summer school. Right? But I've got to tell you something. You'll never guess who's going to be teaching English in summer school."

At this point it finally began to sink in: *This man is not going away.* I realized it was time to make better choices.

I got to work, and you know something? As the year went on John Nicholson not only taught me how to write, he taught me about life. John taught me to look at

> *It began to sink in: This man is not going away.*

my strengths, to believe in myself, to set goals. He showed me how our choices really do shape our destiny. Most of all, he was a teacher who clearly took the time to help.

I went on to college and to graduate school. I went on to write over forty books. When the first one, *Assertive Discipline*, was published,

I wrote this dedication:

> "To John Nicholson. His firm limits and positive warmth and support made this book possible. He truly was the assertive teacher."

Effectiveness Is a Habit You Can Learn

I tell this story to emphasize the importance of your role as a teacher. You may have known a John Nicholson when you were in school—someone who made a difference; someone who affected the direction of your life. The point I'm making is that *you still can fulfill that role today*—in spite of difficult students, class sizes, lack of funding, lack of support. These are tremendous challenges, yes, but there are solutions to them all.

I have had the honor and privilege to study the strategies of teachers who have been recognized as high performers—teachers who bring out the best in their students, who rise above the challenges to go home at the end of each day with a great deal of satisfaction, even gratification from their job. They express their attitudes toward teaching in statements such as these:

If I don't reach out to them, who is going to reach out?

"My class is a last resort with high-school kids. If I don't reach out to them, who is going to reach out? I'm there for them in a way I want to get them to understand. I care about them; I'm concerned about them. I want them to trust me; I want them to trust the system; and in turn I want to educate them."

"Would you want a teacher to give up on *your* child? I go home exhausted because I've tried many, many methods, and sometimes they don't work. But you know, I go back the next day, and I never give up. Because I look in those neat little eyes, and they're saying to me, 'Please help me'—and that's the reason I'm a teacher."

"Two beliefs drive me. One is that every student can learn; the other is that I have the ability to teach every single student."

Here are some of the things that parents, colleagues, counselors and principals have to say about these teachers:

"With his encouragement, he has brought out abilities in my children that they never thought they had. They were able to accomplish things that they never thought they could."

"She can take a failing student and turn him into a very successful student. She will do whatever it takes to make sure a child is successful. She never gives up on a child."

She believes that kids can and will succeed.

"When I think of Jack, I think of someone who can really relate to students, accept them for what they are and move with that—because he honors them and values their individuality."

"She is able to reach students who have had a history of failure and, who many people consider unreachable."

"She gives a little bit of herself to every kid. And the kids know it. Kids want to be with her. They want to be associated with her. I think that's the ultimate compliment for a person."

"Helen is one of those individuals that is just absolutely one hundred percent pro-kid. She believes that kids can and will succeed, so she sets that up as an expectation."

These are not charismatic "super teachers," or teachers who work in upper-middle-class environments with highly-motivated students. These are teachers who face the same types of challenges you do. They come from "urban-impacted" schools surrounded by poverty, drugs, gang violence, the usual assortment of contemporary horrors. They come from communities in which the majority of the students speak English as a second language. They come from situations in which doors have been closed to most students—but they have discovered that by opening those doors, they are able to make a difference. Many of them have come back from near-burnout situations to become outstanding teachers—in some cases, to be named teacher-of-the-year in their school or district.

High-performing teachers all share the same essential attitudes.

What these teachers all have in common is that they have learned that it is their *choice* to be positive. They have learned that they can't sit back and complain or wait for students, parents or "the system" to take action. They know that it is they themselves who must go out and make a difference. They have all *acquired* powerful attributes; they have all *learned* strategies that have empowered them to make a greater difference than they previously thought possible.

As you read this book you'll meet many such teachers. Though their personalities, approaches and teaching environments are varied, these high-performing teachers all share the same essential attitudes and behaviors:

- They have a **mission**. They know exactly what they want to accomplish in the classroom each and every day.

- They have **positive beliefs** in their ability to work successfully with students and to make a difference in their lives.

- They recognize that the **choices** they make have an impact on their success.

- They have well-developed **problem-solving skills** that empower them to create and implement plans for overcoming challenges.

- They have learned how to build **positive relationships with students**, no matter how unmotivated or hostile those students might be.

- They have also learned how to build **positive relationships with parents** in recognition of the crucial role of the home environment in education.

- They maintain a **positive attitude**, understanding that a negative attitude impedes students' learning.

- They understand the necessity of a **support network,** and seek out friends and colleagues who are positive and proactive.

- They have learned how to **plan** their time and effort to make the best use of their skills and resources.

In the following chapters you'll find techniques and strategies for developing these attributes. You'll find numerous examples illustrating how real teachers in real-life situations have successfully learned these skills and applied them.

Right now, though, it's time to focus on *you.*

Get a pencil and a pad of paper and jot down some notes on the questions that follow. Think about your experience as a teacher and your perspective on the challenges you face. Use these notes to design your own individualized approach to developing the skills you will learn in this book.

You'll find techniques for developing these attributes.

- What experiences of your own support the statement, "It's harder to be a teacher today than at any time in our history"?

- What happens to your effectiveness as a teacher if you stop believing that you can make a difference in your students' lives? What is the impact on your students?

- Think about teachers you had as a student who influenced you in the way John Nicholson influenced me. What qualities did these teachers possess that made them effective?

- Think of a student whom you feel you influenced in a positive way. What impact did you have on this student? What approach did you take with this student that was particularly effective?

- What ideals motivated you to become a teacher? To what extent have they been realized? To what extent have they been frustrated? Jot down some specific reasons why you feel your expectations have not been met.

- What aspect of teaching would you most like to change? Do you believe that you can still be successful as a teacher even if this change cannot be made? Why, or why not?

- What changes would you like to achieve in your own effectiveness as a teacher?

What ideals motivated you to become a teacher?

Learning the attributes and strategies of high-performing teachers is no more than a matter of developing new habits of belief, feeling and action. And while no one is entirely comfortable with change, it's easier than you think.

This exercise will demonstrate what I mean: Clasp your hands together with your fingers interlaced. Note whether your left thumb or your right thumb is on top. Chances are that every time you clasp your hands, the same thumb is on top.

Now try it the other way. Open and reclasp your hands, this time with the other thumb on top.

It feels awkward, doesn't it? That's because you've formed the *habit* of doing it the other way. If you're habituated to clasping your hands with your left thumb on top, it feels uncomfortable at first to do it with your right thumb on top.

The key words there are "at first," because if you were consciously to practice doing it with your right thumb on top every day for a period of several weeks, it would become just as comfortable that way as the other way.

That's what change is all about. The more you practice new habits, the more you practice focusing on new ways of thinking and new ways of doing things, the more comfortable you become with them.

That's what *The High-Performing Teacher* is all about: change. It's about recognizing that what's happened in the past does not have to continue in the future. It's about recognizing that you are capable of learning new solutions to the challenges you face.

> *The "High-Performing Teacher" is all about change.*

You *are* capable of changing your life through conscious choice. You are capable of learning to be more successful. You can empower yourself to make a difference in the classroom every day of the year. You can choose to make a difference.

The power is within you to become a more effective teacher. It's up to you to choose to use that power. You owe it to your students to make that choice—and most of all you owe it to yourself.

The Power of Mission

When you walked into your first classroom for the first time, what were the thoughts and aspirations that accompanied you? What motivated you to face a roomful of students who may or may not have had the slightest interest in what you had to offer them?

In brief, why did you become a teacher? What motivated you to take on one of the toughest and most demanding of professions?

If you could go back and reexperience the feelings you had then, chances are you would express them somewhat like this:

- "I want to help children reach their potential."

- "I want to raise their self-esteem."

- "I want to instill in children a sense of lifelong learning."

- "I want to guide them in making their way through the world."

I've heard thoughts like these articulated countless times by beginning and student teachers. You may have expressed it in a slightly different way, but your motivation was probably similar.

You had a mission.

You may not have identified it as such, but you knew what you wanted to accomplish in the classroom. You had a point of focus for your career, a sense of purpose that was the key to your enthusiasm, confidence and optimism.

The problem for many teachers today is that the daily challenges you face can obscure this focus. When you have to navigate your way around difficult students, budget cuts, school violence, contract negotiations, unsupportive parents, paperwork, public and peer negativity and apathetic (even hostile) students, it's easy to lose sight of what you originally wanted to achieve—that overarching goal that inspired and motivated you.

It's easy to get lost among the problems.

Sometimes it may seem accomplishment enough to make it to three o'clock each day, let alone to make a profound difference in students' lives. And that is exactly why so many teachers are frustrated. Stressed. Burned out.

You didn't become a teacher just to make it to the end of the day.

You became a teacher to help students—to enrich their lives. If you've lost sight of this goal among the ever-stiffening challenges you face, no wonder your sense of satisfaction may be fading. No wonder you may go home feeling burned out. Personal satisfaction comes from reaching goals that are important to you. Dissatisfaction arises when these goals seem out of reach or appear to have been replaced by more immediate concerns.

You need to get back in touch with your mission.

But look at it this way: If you're burned out, it follows that at one time you must have been fired up.

To *stay* fired up, to regain the motivation that you knew earlier in your career, to keep that energized feeling every day in the classroom and to bring it home with you each night, you first need to get back in touch with what you want to accomplish, with what originally brought you to teaching.

You need to get back in touch with your mission.

> *The high-performing teacher has a mission and is in touch with that mission at all times.*

Looking Ahead—To Your Retirement Dinner

Here's an activity I use in working with teachers that can help you reacquaint yourself with your mission.

Imagine this scenario: You're at a retirement dinner—your own. You're being honored for a lifetime of contributions as an educator. Attending the event are three of your former students. One by one they stand up and deliver tributes to you.

Now, the question is: *What would you most like to hear your students say?*

Think about it for a moment. How do you want to be remembered?

Personally, I would like to know that I've made a difference in students' lives—that something I'd done or said sparked them to believe that they mattered; that I had inspired them to realize that they could accomplish whatever goals they set for themselves.

To me that's what teaching is all about. John Nicholson was that kind of teacher, and his caring influence affected my entire life. If I were delivering a testimonial for John Nicholson, I wouldn't say, "He taught me how to write a five-page essay" (though I am pleased that he helped me become a better writer). I would say, "He taught me to believe in myself."

So take a few moments to look inside yourself. Think about what you would like to hear former students say about you. Think about the students you're teaching now. What would you want them to say about you at your retirement dinner?

Use the worksheet on the next page to write down your thoughts.

Now reread what you wrote. If you heard your students say these things at your retirement dinner, how would you feel about your career? How would you feel about the way you spent your life?

Satisfied? Proud? Fulfilled? As if everything you did was worthwhile—that you did make a difference?

Isn't this the feeling you want every single teaching day? Isn't this the feeling you want to take home with you every night?

If this feeling is missing, you can get it back. The first step is to write your own mission statement.

Writing Your Personal Mission Statement

The first step is to write your own mission statement.

A mission statement is a basic set of principles, a personal affirmation of your goals and objectives. It is a declaration of purpose, a blueprint for action, a constitution. A mission statement is a guidepost that can help you stay focused on the goals that are most important to you, the goals that will provide you the greatest motivation and bring you the greatest satisfaction as a teacher.

This is how one seventh-grade teacher expresses her mission:

> "My mission as a teacher is to instill in my students a lifelong love of learning—to communicate to them that through learning they can make their dreams come true. I want to help all my students believe in themselves and through that belief reach their highest potential."

What I Would Like My Students to Say About Me at My Retirement Dinner

_____

_____

_____

_____

_____

_____

_____

_____

_____

_____

_____

_____

_____

_____

_____

_____

_____

How do you go about writing your mission statement? This is something you will need to give some thought to. After all, we're talking about an expression of your basic vision, values and direction as a teacher. Don't expect to come up with a concise, definitive answer off the top of your head. One middle-school teacher told me this story about how he came to develop his personal mission statement:

> My school had had a mission statement displayed in the main office for as long as I could remember. I'd read it once or twice without paying much attention to it. About five years ago the principal called a staff meeting to have us write individual mission statements. Well, no one was happy about it. We sat there muttering about how he was always jumping on the latest bandwagon; how instead of wasting our time we could be working on lesson plans or correcting papers.
>
> I wrote that first mission statement because I had to, but it wasn't long before I discovered what a useful tool it is. It helped me rediscover why I became a teacher in the first place. I've revised it many times since then, and I still look at it several times each day. It says:

You'll want to take some time to develop your mission statement.

> "My mission is to build the self-esteem of my students and to help them become independent learners and responsible, self-disciplined individuals. I will respect my students' individual differences and will do everything I can to help them believe in themselves and develop to their full potential. I will grow with my students as I continue to learn from them and from others in the field of education."

You'll want to take some time to develop your mission statement. Write down some preliminary ideas. Review them every day and shift them around in your mind. Think about ways in which you can bring your own attitudes and actions in the classroom into harmony with your goals as a teacher. Jot down a first draft of your mission statement. Continue to analyze, edit and refine it.

Use the insights you gained from the Retirement Dinner activity when you create your personal mission statement. You can draw on other sources as well:

- The examples of personal mission statements quoted in this chapter.

- Reflections on teachers who were your role models during your childhood and your professional training.

- Thoughts about what has been most rewarding to you as a teacher, what has been most frustrating, and what you require from your work in the classroom for self-esteem and personal satisfaction.

- Your life's goals as they relate to your professional goals.

- Insights you have gained during times of quiet reflection into your personal values, strengths and priorities.

Here are a few more sample mission statements that may help you formulate your own:

"My mission is to help each student develop a positive self-image and a sense of self-worth, and to enable each student to reach his or her highest potential—intellectually, socially, emotionally and physically."

"My mission is to raise the self-esteem of my students and to empower them to reach their full potential. Each day, in all interactions with my students, I will treat them with respect, compassion and understanding. I will establish high expectations for them in academics, behavior and peer interactions; and I will hold them responsible for meeting these expectations."

"My mission is to look at each child every day and try to give them what they need to make them believe in themselves. How can I make them feel the best that they can be? How can I give them the skills to beat every challenge? If they don't have that belief, I will work with them until they do. When they walk out of my classroom, I want them to know that they can do it."

"My mission is to empower students to reach a level where they feel they're important. From the first day in September, I work with them to get them to realize that they're okay—that they're important, school is important, education is important—that they have their whole life ahead of them; they can sit there and waste it or they can do something about it."

"My mission is to inspire, to motivate, to enthusiastically give each child a portion of myself so that they can be the best they can be."

"My mission is to help students become active learners in all aspects of their lives; to encourage curiosity, imagination and creativity. I will help students develop self-discipline, responsibility, and good citizenship."

Use the worksheet on the next page to record your own mission statement.

It's rather like signing a contract with yourself.

Why write it down? Having a *written* mission statement forces you to focus on it far more effectively than merely keeping it in your mind. It's rather like signing a contract with yourself—it's a higher level of commitment, a motivation for following through. High-performing teachers write down their mission statement and leave it in a location where they can look at it every day—on their desk, on their bedroom mirror, in their car. That way when the challenges begin to mount, frustration sets in and you begin to doubt your effective-

My Mission Statement

_____

_____

_____

_____

_____

_____

_____

_____

_____

_____

_____

_____

_____

_____

_____

_____

_____

_____

ness as a teacher, you can stay focused by concentrating on your own declaration of purpose.

This story, told to me recently by a fifth-grade teacher, illustrates what I mean:

You have so much to give to your students.

I wrote a note to myself a few years ago at a time when I was so frustrated and discouraged I almost quit. I had a really tough class that year, our teachers' union was about to go out on strike, and I was up for tenure. I knew I loved children, and in my heart I still wanted to be a teacher. So I wrote this note to remind myself why I was there when things got tough. The note read, "You have so much to give to your students. You are a special person that they will remember for listening to them without judging, for helping them see the goodness inside themselves, for showing them they can be whatever they want to be. You are the teacher you would want your child to have."

I'd look at that note several times a day. I couldn't believe how much it helped me get through that awful year. I copied it over and laminated it. I still keep it on my desk where I can see it every day. It's my inspiration. It reminds me why I'm there. No matter what's going on at school, or even in my personal life, when I close the door to my classroom my responsibility is to those kids. They're all that matter. And these words, this mission, has helped me keep in touch with what really makes teaching so worthwhile.

Living Your Mission

With your mission statement before you in the classroom every day, you have a constant reminder of what you're trying to accomplish, of what you're all about as a teacher. It's a giant step toward reaching your full potential, toward being the best teacher you can be.

When you have your mission before you, you plan the day's activities around it. Lesson plans, class assignments, discussions, personal interactions with students all have direction when you use your mission statement as a compass heading.

If you have on your desk a card reminding you of your goal of "motivating, inspiring and transmitting enthusiasm," you will create ways of weaving such objectives into your curriculum.

If every day you read over your words about "critical thinking and problem-solving skills," you will make the extra effort to design lessons that build such skills in every subject area.

If you see before you "...raise my students' self-esteem and treat them with respect and dignity," you will make a point of seeking ways to build relationships with your students, taking an active interest in their success, and giving that extra one-on-one attention to the children who need it.

> *Raise my students self-esteem and treat them with respect and dignity.*

Think of your mission statement as a personal accountability tool. Before you go home at the end of each day, review in your mind everything you did that day to help move you closer to your goals. It takes only a few minutes, and it can leave you feeling positive about yourself and your students:

- I took time out to help April work through her problem with her sister. She appreciated the attention and the advice!

- I praised Salvador for his creativity even though his grammar still needs improvement.

- I followed through with consequences promised to Richard for the choices he made. That was tough, but consistency is crucial if he's going to be the best person he can be.

- I was a little sarcastic with Mindy when she took so long in the restroom. Need to do better tomorrow!

You renew, reenergize and revitalize yourself.

By focusing on motivating, inspiring, and communicating your enthusiasm to students every day, you renew, reenergize and revitalize yourself—not only daily but hourly, minute by minute. Here's what two teachers whose mission statements are quoted earlier in this chapter have to say about this "what's-in-it-for-me" aspect of their mission:

> "It's the kids that keep me going. I get my energy from them. When I'm focused on my mission, I'm doing the things that reignite my enthusiasm and keep me alive in my profession. When the kids are feeling good and meeting with success, I'm feeling successful. What comes back to me from the kids refuels me, energizes me, and keeps me going."

> "My mission as a teacher is to get [students] to believe in themselves, but it isn't altogether altruistic. It keeps me on target. I walk out of school every day feeling very up. I feel good about what I did, and I feel good about coming back the next day."

It all comes back to what we talked about in the first chapter—it's you who has the power to make a difference. Having a mission statement is the first step toward increasing your effectiveness in the classroom. When the challenges start mounting, your mission statement will remind you that you're there to make a difference—that you *do* make a difference. In turn, knowing that you're fulfilling your mission every day, even in small increments, can't help but raise your self-esteem and leave you eager to face the challenges the next day will bring.

The Power of Belief

If you *believe* you can be a high-performing teacher, you're halfway to being one—and maybe even a step beyond. Simply by holding and acting on positive beliefs, you can empower yourself to achieve success in the classroom.

Effective teachers believe that students can learn and succeed. They believe that they can help students learn and succeed. More importantly, they believe absolutely that *they* can achieve the goals that will bring satisfaction and a sense of accomplishment—that they can live their mission in the classroom every day of the year.

When I raise this point in conversations with teachers, I'm generally greeted by a few raised eyebrows. So before we go further now, it's important for you to understand something about beliefs. Beliefs are not just passive thoughts. *Beliefs create self-fulfilling prophecies.* What you believe to be true *is* true, as far as your feelings and actions are concerned.

If you believe you can't, you can't.

If you believe you can, you can.

Beliefs drive achievement. This idea has revolutionized the study and practice of psychology. It has gained acceptance in such diverse fields as business, sports, politics—and education. To illustrate, some years ago a team of Harvard researchers under the direction of Robert Rosenthal conducted a study that became known as "Pygmalion in the Classroom." They went into a school and selected 90 students of average ability and three teachers whose classes over the last three years had achieved average results. Each teacher was assigned a class of 30 students for the coming school year. The teachers were told that these were gifted children. The researchers told them, "You were chosen for this assignment because you have demonstrated superior ability and because we know you can bring out the greatest potential in these children."

At the end of the school year, the progress of the students was tested. The result? Their academic performance had soared.

Again, these were average students and average teachers. The only above-average factor was *what the teachers believed.*

You too have the power to achieve spectacular results in the classroom—simply by choosing to believe in your ability to do it.

> *The high-performing teacher believes*
> *that he or she can be successful*
> *with students.*

Why Negative Beliefs Cause Negative Results

The reason this is so has to do with the way we human beings form habits. Any negative belief—the belief that students can't learn; the belief that nothing you can do can make a difference—is something you have habitually *learned* to believe. As the "Pygmalion" study proves, such a belief may not necessarily have anything to do with reality. But once a negative belief becomes a habit, you tend to act *as if* it were true. The results of your actions in turn negatively impact your feelings about teaching.

Why are so many teachers today hampered by negative beliefs? One big reason has to do with current public attitudes toward education. Over and over we hear it said that today's kids are unteachable, that people have lost faith in the schools, that "teachers just aren't doing their job."

Then there are newspapers, magazines and TV. Hardly a week goes by that a story doesn't appear about "the failures of education," about rising illiteracy rates, about standardized test scores reaching another record low.

We hear it said that today's kids are unreachable.

But why blame society or the media? If you want to pinpoint an all-too-common source of this negativity, you don't have to look any further than some of your own colleagues. How many of the following do you hear spoken at your school during the course of a typical week?

- "Forget it. It's impossible with these kids."

- "Ever try *talking* to some of these parents?"

- "You hear what our principal wants us to do now?"

- "Was your day as bad as mine? I can't do a thing with these kids. They don't listen; they don't learn; they don't care."

- "This place is a zoo."

When you're bombarded with comments like these day in and day out, it's easy to feel that the situation is hopeless. Without even realizing it, you can form the habit of believing that nothing you do can make a difference.

Such a belief inevitably and immediately affects your focus. For example, if you walk into the classroom believing that your students can't do the work, what happens next? You create a self-fulfilling prophecy. If you believe that students can't do the work, you'll focus on those children who *aren't* doing it. And so when a child has trouble, it's easy to think, "Just as I thought: *These kids can't do the work."*

This attitude in turn conditions your actions. Here's what I mean: If you believe a child really can't learn, you instinctively won't make as great an effort to teach her. There's a voice in your mind saying, "She really can't learn, she really can't learn, she really can't learn." So you may make a halfhearted attempt and quickly give up—without even realizing that's what you're doing!

Attitude affects actions, which in turn affect your feelings. If your *mission* is to help students reach their potential but your *actions* reflect the belief that they can't learn, you're constantly aware that you're not fulfilling your mission—that you *can't* fulfill your mission. You feel like a failure in the classroom—day after day. You go home feeling frustrated and burned out—day after day.

> *Attitude affects actions, which in turn affect your feelings.*

You can see how this process works by assessing your own negative beliefs—and the consequences of those beliefs. Take time out now and complete the chart on the facing page by adding two more examples in the space provided.

- First, write a negative belief you hold.

- In the next column write down what you inevitably focus on because of this belief.

- Then, write the actions your belief prompts you to take.

- In the final column write the feelings that result from these actions.

If you believe you can't, you can't.

Negative Beliefs			
Negative belief:	**Because of this belief your focus is on:**	**Because of this belief you take these actions:**	**Feelings that result:**
Students can't learn.	Students who have trouble learning.	Make a weak effort to help, then give up.	Frustration.

Positive Beliefs Can Yield Positive Results

Positive beliefs, however, create *positive* self-fulfilling prophecies. For example, a belief that your students *can* learn will have a positive effect on your focus. You'll go into the classroom looking for students who respond to your efforts: "I can teach these kids. Way to go, Joaquin, you're getting it. Hey, Barbara, that's the way. Wonderful improvement since your last test."

When you focus on positive results, your actions are affected positively as well. If Chris isn't quite up to the standards of Joaquin or Barbara, you'll keep trying with him. If one method doesn't work, you'll try another. *The key to success is your conscious, positive thoughts:* "Hey, he can *learn*. Just keep after it, and you'll find a solution that works for him."

> *If one method doesn't work, you'll try another.*

And what happens when you find that your actions have been successful? You go home *feeling* successful and anticipating more successes every day. Of course you feel good. You're fulfilling your mission!

Now take a few minutes and complete the chart on the facing page. Restate the negative beliefs you listed on the previous chart as positive beliefs and add the likely consequences of such beliefs.

If you believe you can, you can.

High-performing teachers recognize the power of their beliefs. They have high expectations for themselves and for their students. And these expectations are reflected in their actions in the classroom every day. When you listen to high-performing teachers talk about their work, you hear statements like these:

> "I believe that every child can learn regardless of the baggage they bring with them into my classroom or the kind of morning they had or what's going on at home. I accept no excuses from them, because I know that they can do it."

Positive Beliefs			
Positive belief:	Because of this belief your focus is on:	Because of this belief you take these actions.	Feelings that result:
Students can learn.	Students who show that they have learned.	Keep trying with other students.	Satisfaction. Motivation.

"My beliefs in what education is all about enable me to have high expectations in my classroom, to expect the most from those children and to pull it right out of them. I try not to let one situation go by without leading it in the right direction and turning it into a positive experience."

It's the standard I have set. I believe in them.

"It all comes down to expectations. I believe my students can behave. They do behave. It's the standard I have set. I believe in them. They believe in themselves. They trust me. They see it. They know I care. It's done. In this room, there is appropriate behavior."

A letter I received from a second-grade teacher demonstrates dramatically how positive beliefs yield positive results. "Damian came to me with practically no reading or writing skills," this teacher wrote:

He was extremely quiet and withdrawn. The first day of school his first-grade teacher warned me how Damian would just sit at his desk "spacing out" all day, how she had let him "do his own thing" because he just couldn't do the work.

It was my first year of teaching, and my initial reaction was, "What am I going to do with a kid like that?" Then I said to myself, "Maybe she just didn't give him a chance." I was so new, I thought maybe I was being idealistic and naive. Here I was fresh out of college and taking on a challenge that this experienced teacher had given up on, but I did everything I could to teach Damian how to read. I made it my special project to motivate him and get him to do it. As a result we both learned a lot, and we both had a lot of fun in the process. By the end of the year he was reading on a 1_2 level, writing and illustrating little stories, and writing to me in his journal every day. His parents were so grateful, and Damian became a notice-ably happier child that year.

I'm glad this happened early in my teaching career, before I had the chance to get disillusioned. The experience taught me never to doubt my ability to teach a child.

Never doubt your ability—to teach a child, to enforce behavior, to get parents involved, to overcome any challenge. Your beliefs can empower you to make a differ-ence, or they can disempower you and hinder your success. The choice is yours.

> *Never doubt your ability to teach a child.*

Take a moment now to think about that statement: *The choice is yours.*

This is important because every one of us is capable of changing our beliefs.

How to Change Your Beliefs from Negative to Positive

Like many teachers, you probably have some negative beliefs that are standing in the way of your success and satisfaction. How can you turn these beliefs around?

There are four steps to follow in changing your beliefs:

1. Become aware of your negative beliefs.

2. Recognize your power to change those beliefs.

3. Model the attitudes of high-performing teachers.

4 Recognize the consequences of your negative beliefs.

Take a close look at your beliefs. What negative beliefs are you consciously aware of bringing into the classroom, beliefs that may be keeping you from fulfilling your mission? Search inside and be very honest with yourself. Do any of these sound like you?

- "These kids aren't interested in learning."

- "These parents just don't care."

- "I can't teach these students."

- "The administration won't back me up."

- "I can't get Heather to behave; she's incorrigible."

- "The community environment is hopeless; how can one teacher make a difference?

- "I can't do this. Teaching is too hard for me."

Now, what about the negative beliefs that you *aren't* consciously aware of? Try an experiment for a week: Keep a pad of paper in your pocket or purse and beside your bed. Pay attention to the thoughts running through your mind as you go through the day. Every time you're aware of a negative thought about your effectiveness—"I can't do anything about Monica's disruptions; just ignore her and wait for the bell to ring"; "I'm wasting my time trying to teach Robert"—jot it down.

After a week, you should have a clear picture of the beliefs that may be keeping you from being the teacher you would like to be. Make a list of the negative beliefs that you would like to change.

You do have the power to become positive and enthusiastic. Next, you need to have the *conviction* that you truly can change your beliefs. To help raise that conviction let me tell you that you do have the power to become positive and enthusiastic about your ability to fulfill your mission. I can make this statement with confidence because so many teachers I know have done it. *Many teachers who today we would consider "superstars" of their profession at one time held negative beliefs about their ability to do the job.*

For some such teachers, an unexpected success with one student leads them to believe that they can succeed with others. "When I was assigned to a high school in the city," one school teacher told me:

> I burned out almost before I started. The school was your basic urban nightmare—gangs, drugs, racial fights, welfare families with absentee fathers and addict mothers. Half the kids in my eleventh-grade history classes were reading below fifth-grade level. The principal seemed more interested in pretending there were no problems than in supporting teachers' efforts to do something about them. Getting kids to learn under such conditions was like bailing out the ocean with a seashell. After a few weeks I stopped trying. I was mired in all the negativity. I would walk into the classroom every day looking for things to not go right.
>
> One student—a quiet boy named David, who hadn't distinguished himself except perhaps by his quietness—came to me after class one
>
> *I was mired in all the negativity.*
>
> day and asked me if I'd write a recommendation for a part-time job at a TV station. It was maintenance work—emptying wastebaskets and so on—but David added that he wanted eventually to work in TV as a newsman and hoped that the job would give him a foot in the door.
>
> That caught my attention. Here was a kid who couldn't write a paragraph without misspelling every third word, yet he had set his sights on a career as a journalist. I had written him off just as I had written off so many others. He had a long, uphill road to travel, but he hadn't given up on himself.
>
> I started giving David more attention, encouraging him to express himself in class, helping him with his written work. It soon became clear to me that I was being unfair

to the other students—how many more Davids might there be out there?—and so I began spreading my attention around. Sure, a lot of the kids resisted, but there were quite a few who responded positively to my positive interest. To keep a long story short, once I started *believing* that I could make a difference for my students, I found that I actually could.

For other teachers, having a positive experience with a student other teachers have written off can shift their perspective. "I didn't know anything about Stuart when he was assigned to me," one such teacher related to me recently:

> This was my first permanent teaching job after two years as a sub, and Stuart's was just one face among thirty-three in my fourth-grade class. The first day I had to talk to him about karate-kicking the doors and making a mess around his desk by cutting up paper into confetti. I kept him after class to talk to him privately about my expectations for his behavior, and I found him an engaging young boy. He seemed in no hurry to get home, and he started telling me wild stories about himself as a superhero, an ally of the Teenage Mutant Ninja Turtles. These were fantasies I associated with much younger children. I encouraged him to write down his stories, and he did, illustrating them with felt-tipped pens.

It taught me to have high expectations for all my students.

It was maybe a month later that another teacher said, "I understand you've got Stuart in your class. What a way to break in a new teacher! How do you keep your sanity?" I was surprised to learn that Stuart had a negative reputation going back to kindergarten. I'd found him to be less mature than most of his classmates, more apt than most to talk out of turn or shoot up out of his seat, but not especially a problem. I had no idea what I'd been doing right, but I thought that as long as it worked I'd keep on doing it.

I concluded that not having negative expectations about Stuart's behavior had a lot to do with my success with him. It was the most valuable lesson a beginning teacher could have learned. It taught me to have high expectations for *all* my students.

If these teachers could fulfill their mission after developing positive beliefs, why not you?

Please understand: Positive beliefs aren't all that's required to be a high-performing teacher. There are skills involved too. But the skills you need to raise your effectiveness are within your reach. *Every "you" reading this book can learn or revitalize these skills.*

> *The skills you need are within your reach.*

The way you acquire them is by modeling the attitudes and actions of high-performing teachers:

- by choosing to respond to challenges instead of being frustrated by them.

- by seeking creative solutions to problems and accepting the risks that may be necessary to pursue them.

- by "going the distance" in reaching out to students and enlisting the support of parents.

- by finding and focusing on their students' strengths.

- by finding ways to coordinate these qualities in a plan of action for fulfillment of their mission.

These are all skills you'll be reading about in subsequent chapters of this book. By acquiring these skills, and by modeling the ways that high-performing teachers apply them, you'll get the same results they do.

—*If* you have high expectations of success, that is.

If you start with negative beliefs, chances are you won't take the trouble to acquire or apply the necessary skills. If you "know" the results will be negative, what's the point of putting out the extra effort?

But if you start with positive beliefs—if you believe that you can make a difference—you'll settle for nothing less than positive results. Here is an example of how one teacher, distinguished from her colleagues mainly by her expectations of success, handled a complex learning and behavior problem:

You'll settle for nothing less than positive results.

Last year there was a girl in my class named Mary, a tough, defiant, uncooperative kid, highly unmotivated to learn. She started out in another third-grade class and was moved into mine because her original teacher couldn't handle her. This teacher seemed to be in a battle with Mary every time I walked past her classroom. Once I saw her slam a yardstick on a table next to Mary's desk, "to startle some sense into her," as she told me later."

Not long after this the decision was made to transfer Mary to my class. It happened very suddenly, and I never found out why. All I knew was that now I was the one who had to find a way of working with Mary.

She came from a dysfunctional home environment. She had a very limited vocabulary and poor verbal skills—she didn't know the names of common household objects. She had acquired few social skills either. She was physically aggressive toward other children and did not socialize with them at all. She had no regard for authority and refused to do what she was told. She continually got out of her seat and wandered around the classroom. I had never seen her smile.

I didn't know where to start, but I really believed I could

make progress with Mary. This belief was what brought me the success I later experienced. I saw her as a child who severely lacked nurturing. I felt that if I could build a relationship with her, make her feel safe and get her to trust me, then we could get on with basic social and academic skills.

I spent time talking to Mary each day. I'd ask her to do small tasks for me, and I gave her choices—not for the sake of avoiding consequences but for being the one in control. That became the key. Mary resented being told what to do, but she enjoyed the power of making her own choices. One day, for instance, the class was making posters and Mary was just wandering around. I asked her to return to her seat, and she just looked away and continued walking toward the back of the classroom. I walked up to her slowly and said, "Mary, you know what you're supposed to be doing. I'm not going to tell you what to do. You're in control of Mary; you can tell yourself what to do." After about 15 seconds, Mary returned to her seat and went to work. I gave her a sticker to add positive reinforcement to what we had started. And I said, "I really like having you in my class. Let's see this poster...."

Mary's progress was slow, but little by little she came around. It took a lot of patience, but mostly it took not backing down on my belief that she could learn to behave in my

> *I really believed I could make progress with Mary.*

classroom. I just had to keep telling myself, "She can do it. She can do it." And I know it's because of this belief that Mary came through—with good choices and even an occasional smile that she could no longer hold back.

Finally, consider the consequences of your negative beliefs. Negative beliefs actually *give you permission not to try*—to write students off, to sweep them under the rug, to accept the status quo. When you think about it this way, you can't help but recognize what a terrible injustice it is to the child.

But just as important, it's an injustice to *you*.

Think of the price you pay for your negative beliefs. Consider the effect on your career if you go home every day telling yourself, "I can't do my job." In a very short time you will come to feel emotionally exhausted. Burned out.

> *You have to believe there's hope.*

Consider the impact of such beliefs on your self-esteem. You *have* to believe there's hope; otherwise you're conceding that you're never going to succeed. That's a demoralizing load to carry. Isn't that reason enough to change your beliefs—to raise your expectations of success?

Beliefs and skills—you need both if you're going to fulfill your mission. But beliefs come first.

The Power of Choice

Maintaining positive beliefs is essential to your effectiveness in the classroom. That's why it's crucial to hold on to these beliefs in the face of challenges. And make no mistake about it: Your beliefs *will* be challenged.

"I was the Charlie Hustle of teachers when I first started," an eighth-grade teacher once told me:

> I was really confident in my ability to succeed in the classroom. Then came the first day of school. I believed I could reach any student with enough individual attention; but I started with thirty-three kids, and before the first day was over the administration transferred in eight more. I believed I could motivate students, but when I gave my first assignment this one belligerent student slouched in his seat, glared at me, and said, "You can't make me do anything." I believed I could work out any problem with a student as long as I had parents' support, but I soon discovered that parents would find excuse after excuse not to come to conferences. Until I wised up, I didn't know what to do with these challenges. All I knew was that nothing about teaching was the way it should be.

There is a choice all teachers face today: You can choose to be overwhelmed by the challenges that inevitably arise, or you can choose to find strategies that will help you overcome them. Any time your belief in your ability to fulfill your mission is challenged, you must be aware that you have this choice.

Like the teacher whose story I just quoted, you probably feel that you shouldn't *have* to struggle against challenges all the time. And you're right. Students *should* be motivated. Administrators *should* keep class sizes down. Parents *should* be supportive. Children *should* be respectful and well-behaved. You *should* have adequate planning time, up-to-date textbooks, ample supplies.

All those "shoulds" are absolutely correct. The problem is that they can also be impediments to you. If you look at them closely, you will see that underlying each one is the belief that things ought to be different. Unfortunately that belief won't get you anywhere. Whenever your belief of what *should* be is in conflict with what *is*, you're going to end up feeling frustrated.

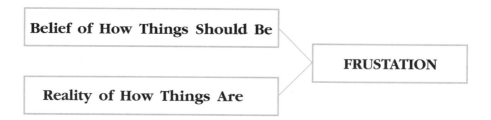

That's what frustration is: a gap between expectation and reality. When traffic on the interstate should be going fifty-five miles per hour but it's creeping along at twenty, you feel frustrated. When the supermarket checkout line should be moving but there's someone up there arguing about coupons, you feel frustrated. Any time you believe that things have to be different for you to reach your goal, you're going to feel frustrated. Trapped. Disempowered.

The truth is, all your "shoulds" probably are one-hundred-percent correct. The reality is that many aspects of teaching today aren't the way they should be. No one can fault you for feeling frustrated. The question is, what are you going to do about it? Remain frustrated and accept dissatisfaction? Or choose to be different?

That brings us back to the issue of choice. The choices we make about the challenges we face shape our destiny.

Let's give that last statement a closer look: *The choices we make about the challenges we face shape our destiny*. You can choose to stay with the "shoulds" and remain frustrated. Or, you can choose to look at things the way they really are and seek solutions that move you toward fulfillment of your mission.

Think of it as a responsibility—a *response-ability*. You have the *ability* to choose your *response* to the challenges. If you take the position that you should not have to deal with them, you become a victim. *You choose to* make *yourself a victim*. You end up frustrated, bitter, burned out. You give up.

But if you choose to respond realistically to the challenges, you can find a way to confront them that preserves your self-esteem and keeps you focused on your mission.

> *The high-performing teacher recognizes that he or she has a choice about how to respond to the challenges that arise.*

Identifying Your Choices

When you believe in your mission, you *want* to find ways of rising above the challenges. The hardest problem you may face is in recognizing that you do indeed have a choice. One teacher, recognized for her effectiveness in working with middle-school students in an environment plagued by the entire range of challenges, explains her choice this way:

I work with high-risk students in a high-risk community. And within that community are even higher-risk students. My responsibility is to work with those students. I don't

It's my choice.
It's my challenge.
It's my love.

get rid of them because they don't fit the typical high-risk profile. They are mine when I meet them in September, and my responsibility is to see them through to June, whatever it takes. I have choices. I can work with these young people, or I can pass them on. I choose to work with them. It's my choice. It's my challenge. It's my love. It's what keeps me going. I need the challenge. I need to see young people understanding themselves. I take the time. I choose to take the time. I want to take the time.

Another teacher had to face the challenge of a variety of behavior-related problems brought about by a lack of home discipline. Here's how she explains her choice:

It's so easy to let outside factors influence what goes on inside the classroom. It would be very easy to say, "I give up. This is too tough for me. These kids are not behaving." But I've made a personal decision to focus on what's going on in my classroom, and if I'm going to have control in my room, I need to teach behavior, to give these kids things that they haven't gotten by the time they come to me. I can't control what goes on outside my classroom, but I can control what goes on inside my classroom. I expect self-control in behavior from my students. I've made a personal choice to do that and I work darn hard at it.

Your choice may present itself in many ways—the choice to seek a new teaching strategy, investigate a new curriculum, or find a new way of approaching students who are unmotivated or who display behavior problems.

The key is to recognize that you *have* the choice to take a new action.

This recognition requires a *paradigm shift*—a fundamental change in perception that makes available a new range of possibilities. In his book *The Seven Habits of Highly Effective People*, Stephen R. Covey calls this shift "the 'Aha!' experience—when someone finally sees the composite picture in another way...as though a light were suddenly turned on inside."

Paradigm shifts were behind the American framers' proposition that personal liberty was a higher value than the rights of kings, behind Pasteur's discovery that infections were spread by bacteria, behind railroad builders' disregard of the prevalent belief that traveling at speeds greater than thirty miles per hour would kill a human being. In each case a long-entrenched way of looking at things was challenged and set aside in favor of a new model. The results were new attitudes, actions and energies.

Making a paradigm shift can be as simple as choosing to look for a solution instead of assuming there isn't one. Often, as Covey puts it, "The way we see the problem *is* the

> *The way we see the problem is the problem.*

problem." Whatever the specifics might be, your paradigm shift will involve recognizing that *the responsibility for reaching students rests with you and not with them*.

One teacher who has worked with us gives this account of how such a change in perception saved her career:

> When I first started teaching back in 1973, I went in (as I think most teachers do) with great aspirations and goals of changing the world, and what I found in the classroom was a real surprise. I experienced frustration. I experienced anger. It wasn't at all what I thought it was going to be. Not only weren't my lesson plans working; I was not touching the kids. I was not reaching them. There

was a wall between us, and the easiest response was to blame them for putting it up, for not being the type of students I thought they should be. I was seeing *them* as the problem, seeing the barriers between us as something I couldn't control.

I had to decide whether this was really the profession I wanted to be in. What happened was that I finally told myself, wait a minute, let's take a look at the person in the mirror. And when I did that, what I realized was that the kids weren't going to magically change—that *I* was going to have to change or else get out. And that meant making some choices within myself. One thing I did was to think back to my own high-school days and ask myself what it had been that made me listen to a teacher. And a quote came to mind: "Kids don't care how much you know until they know how much you care." And I thought: I'm not teaching English, I'm teaching individual students who have to know that I care.

I was going to have to change or else get out.

When I look back, it's scary to think that I could still be where I was, seeing kids as the problem, seeing the barriers as something beyond my control. I have seen many excellent colleagues who got out of the profession because they got burned out before they could see that they had that choice.

For other teachers the paradigm shift may come about through a rewarding experience with a student, a teacher support-network meeting, a seminar, or, as in the case of this Florida teacher, a word of advice from someone who has experienced such a shift:

I've been a teacher since 1964, but nine years ago I was ready to quit. I'd always been a firm believer in homework, but my sixth-graders seemed to regard it as an infringement on their rights. Oh, there were a few kids whose parents got on their cases, and others who made a sort of halfhearted effort, but most of them would not do any homework at all. They'd even stopped giving me the usual the-dog-ate-it excuses. They just would not do it.

I felt discouraged, even humiliated. Then one of the younger teachers, whom I didn't know very well, asked me for a ride home one afternoon when her car wouldn't start. I'd had a particularly bad day, and I found myself opening up to her about the problem. She said something like, "Maybe the problem is with your expectations. You want things to still be the way they were when you started teaching."

I needed to try something different.

I'm afraid I said something snappish back at her—it sounded like she was telling me I was old and behind the times. "All I meant," she said, "is that I had to deal with this issue when I first started teaching, and I didn't get anywhere as long as I kept thinking kids *ought* to be motivated to do homework. I'd read all the same studies you have about the importance of homework, and I finally came to the conclusion that I needed to try something different."

I thought about that all week. I thought about it *a lot.* She was right; I'd been banging my head against a wall when I should have been looking around for doors. That night I started jotting down some ideas about how I might do things differently. It took me most of the semester to get a successful plan going, but the thought that there were things I *could do* was all it took to get me started.

Choosing to Make That Extra Effort

The choices you make in the face of challenges can mean the difference between the success and failure of your mission. If you truly believe your *students* have to change in order for you to fulfill your mission; if you have to wait for parents, administrators or society to change, *you completely disempower yourself.*

If you choose to change, you can revitalize your career. If you con-

> *If you choose to change, you can revitalize your career.*

tinue to complain about the way things should be, you remain on the downhill slide toward burnout. "I've been teaching in my community for seventeen years," a teacher from San Diego told us recently:

> But in the past few years, there's been a tremendous increase in students who speak little or no English. This year I was assigned six LEP [limited-English proficient] students, and I just couldn't seem to get through to them. They were very quiet, polite and obedient, but they'd look at me with a blank stare as though they didn't understand a word I was saying—and in fact they didn't. The ESL [English as a second language] specialist was coming into my room forty-five minutes a day, but it just wasn't enough. I felt frustrated because I didn't know what to do. I was angry because it seemed unfair that I should have to teach so many students with such a wide variation in skills and abilities. Most of all I felt inadequate because although I'd always thought of myself as a good teacher, I knew I wasn't giving these kids what they needed.

> I was sharing gripes about this problem with other teachers, and one of them mentioned a weekend class that was being offered that month by a local college. She had taken it last year, she said, and it had really helped her out. She had seven ESL students this year, and the strategies she had learned in the class were making her job with them a lot easier.

> I decided right away that I wanted to take the class, and I suggested to two other frustrated colleagues that we take it together. One of them said something about being

busy that weekend, and the other said she wasn't going to use her weekend time to work and not get paid for it. Their attitude really dampened my enthusiasm, but when I thought about it, I realized that here was this opportunity to do something about the situation instead of complaining about it.

Taking that class turned out to be one of the wisest choices I'd ever made. Not only did I learn ways to work with LEP students, I started sharing ideas and experiences with the teacher who told me about the class. We now have my fifth-graders and her third-graders getting together for cross-age tutoring and other cooperative activities. Our principal is sending us both to another workshop on the subject, and we'll be responsible for presenting the material to the staff when we get back. I still hear those two teachers who didn't take the class making excuses about the situation and complaining that they shouldn't have to deal with it. I hope we'll be able to motivate them—it sure was satisfying to discover that *I* could still be motivated to try something new.

> *I could still be motivated to try something new.*

Choosing to overcome a challenge always involves making an extra effort. The teacher quoted in the last example chose to take the trouble to learn new skills. You may find that a concentrated application of skills you already have may be all you need. Either way, the contrast in results between the teacher who chooses to confront the challenges and the one who opts for the *status quo* can be dramatic—as this middle-school teacher learned:

Michael's reputation as a difficult student goes way back. I'd heard other teachers talk about how lazy and disruptive he is. When I saw his name on my class list this year, I knew I'd have to make some important choices in order to make this year the best year it could be—for Michael and for me.

I made three conscious choices which I think made a difference. The first was to build a trusting and positive relationship with Michael. The second was to make it clear to him that I cared enough about him not to accept or make excuses for his inappropriate work habits and behavior. And the third was not to give up on Michael no matter what he might say or do.

I made three conscious choices which I think made a difference.

It meant a lot of hard work and extra effort. I'd phone Michael a few times a week to talk to him about how things were going. Once I even went to his home to help him with a project he was doing for another class. He began to see that I genuinely cared about him, that he wasn't just a faceless student to me. He was a human being whom I found to be interesting, capable, and fun to be with.

Now our relationship lets us get down to business. We're more focused on learning. Michael has become sort of a Dr. Jekyll and Mr. Hyde. In my class he follows directions, participates in class discussions and completes his work. He's beginning to show a real interest in the literature we read. But all I hear from other teachers is what trouble he is.

Often when you chose to make the extra effort to overcome a challenge, you will find unexpected rewards. This was the case of a high-school history teacher who returned to the classroom after an absence of several years:

I welcomed the challenge of teaching in an ethnically diverse school. The community had some of the usual urban problems, but it was not a slum. There was a strong middle-class element and an encouraging representation of motivated students.

The problem was the textbook. The kids in my classes were about sixty percent African American and thirty percent Japanese- and Korean-American, but the text had nothing on black history between slavery and Martin Luther King and nothing on Asian history at all. The kids were resentful, and so was I. Since there was no money in the budget for alternative learning materials, I decided to create my own. I called up some professors at the state university, and I found them eager to help. They gave me lists of books, many of which were in the public library. This was before home computers were common, and I typed my materials on duplicating masters and ran them off on the school's machine.

The kids were really responsive. That first year I got two students who'd always taken the history-is-boring line fired up enough to sign up for the College Board history exam. The next year I enlisted some other teachers to prepare alternative materials with me on a cooperative basis. I'm still using these and other self-created materials in my classes—and as a result of my initiative I've also hooked on as a paid consultant to two textbook publishers.

What Choices Are Within Your Power?

In this chapter you've read the personal accounts of teachers who:

- were confronted by challenges that compromised their belief that they could fulfill their mission.

- recognized that they had the power to choose between a "should" response and a pragmatic response to the situation.

- created a plan for confronting the challenge and made the necessary effort to implement their plan.

With these examples as background, it's time now to apply the power of choice to your own situation. Get a pad of paper and a pen and start thinking about your own challenges and how you might choose to respond to them. Using a separate sheet of paper for each challenge, follow these procedures:

1. Describe the situation.

2. Write your "should" response to the situation (how you think things "should" be).

3. Identify the reality you face that makes "should" an ineffective response.

4. Based on the reality, list three different actions you could take in response to the challenge.

Keep yourself on a path toward fulfillment of your mission.

Above all, recognize that in each such situation you *have* a choice. You can dwell on the "shoulds" and feel frustrated, angry, ineffectual. Or, you can accept the reality that the challenges aren't going away and find new responses that keep your positive beliefs intact and yourself on a path toward fulfillment of your mission.

You can't change your students. You can't change their parents, the educational system or "society." But you can change your own responses. And the choice to change is a choice against frustration and for empowerment.

The Power of Overcoming Challenges

If you want to live your mission, you need to learn ways to rise above the challenges. In the last chapter we talked about choosing to respond to challenges instead of letting them frustrate you. In this chapter we consider what responses you choose.

Often teachers address problems with the same responses they've been using for twenty years. They use the techniques they learned in college, the ones recommended by other teachers, the ones they read about in education journals—all the methods that have worked in the past. The trouble is, they're not working now.

It's another "should" situation. If you choose an approach simply because you feel it should work, you get the same result anyone experiences who goes by "shoulds": frustration.

For example, let's say you're having a problem with students who won't complete assignments. You keep them in from recess. You keep them after school to finish their work. You send notes home to their parents. And still the students won't work. They don't seem to care about anything that goes on in class. You're frustrated. So you keep them in from recess. You keep them after school. You send notes home. And they still don't work, and you're still frustrated. So you keep them in from recess . . .

See what I mean?

High-performing teachers go a step further. When faced with a challenge, they look at what they've done and gauge whether it's working. If it isn't, they try something different. And if that doesn't work, they look for something else. They keep trying new solutions until they find one that works.

And they take risks. High-performing teachers would agree with a colleague of mine, a business consultant who maintains that the main difference between winners and losers is that winners lose more often than losers. They also win far more often, because instead of becoming frustrated and giving up, they use negative results as steppingstones toward their mission. They have their eye on their goal at all times, and they are willing to accept a setback if it helps them find a surer path to that goal.

> *The high-performing teacher looks for creative solutions to problems that could compromise his or her mission.*

How to Identify Your Problem Situations

Let's assume you've made the paradigm shift we talked about in the last chapter. You know that you can choose to address a challenge rather than let it frustrate you. How do you go about doing it?

You begin by looking at the problems you are facing, the responses you are currently making to them, and the outcomes you are experiencing. There are four steps to this procedure:

1. Recognize that there is a challenge.

2. Determine whether you have any potential influence over the challenge.

My Challenges

_____

_____

_____

_____

_____

_____

_____

_____

_____

_____

_____

_____

_____

_____

_____

_____

_____

_____

3. Identify the responses you have already made.

4. Assess the outcomes of your responses.

How can you tell when you are facing a challenge? There is one certain clue: our old friend frustration. Frustration is a red flag that tells you you've got a problem. If you feel frustrated, chances are you've been unsuccessfully dealing with the problem for some time. You think about it a great deal. You talk about it in the teachers' lounge and complain about it at home.

If you give it some thought, you can identify your challenge and give it a name. Very likely you can name several challenges. Take a moment now and jot them down on the worksheet on the preceding page for future reference.

Now let's look at the second step: Ask yourself, "Is there anything I can do to change this situation? Is there action I can take now that will help me solve this problem in the short term?"

There are some challenges over which you have little or no control—class size, school-board membership or students' home environment, for example. With challenges such as these, the best way to avoid frustration is to accept reality and recognize that your potential influence is limited. Go back to your list of challenges and cross out all that fall into this category.

The challenges that warrant your efforts are the ones that you can potentially influence—challenges such as "students won't work," for example, or "Donna's constant backtalk." These are the problems for which you are capable of finding effective solutions.

Most likely you've been trying to find solutions to them for a while. The third step then is to identify the actions you've already taken in response to a challenge. For example:

Challenge	Responses
Students won't work	Kept them in at recess
	Kept them after school
	Sent notes home
	Called parents

The fourth step is to assess your results. What has happened as a result of all your responses? Was the problem solved?

If not, how do you feel? If you've been assuming that your responses should work, you know very well how you feel:

Challenge:	Students won't work
Responses	**Outcome**
Kept them in at recess	Students still won't work
Kept them after school	Students still won't work
Sent notes home	Students still won't work
Called parents	Students still won't work
	Still frustrated

Please notice that all the responses in this example are good, valid responses to the problem. They're the classic responses you have learned that have worked well in the past. But if they don't work now, it's time to stop using them over and over in the expectation that they should work.

Finding Solutions to Your Challenges

Once again, the first key to finding answers that work is to accept reality. If the tried-and-true answers are proving to be tried and *false*, you need to find new ones.

> ***Try new methods until you fnd one that works.***

If your problem is students who won't work, you may need to set up a motivational system and award stickers, free time or "no-homework" passes for assignments completed.

If your problem is students who won't listen, you may need to try cooperative learning groups instead of lecturing to the whole class.

If your problem involves individual learning or behavior difficulties, you may need to set up a peer-tutoring system or send home notes to parents every day.

Whatever the problem may be, recognize that you must live in the present. When traditional methods prove ineffective, don't just keep recycling them until frustration sets in. Instead, try new methods until you find one that works.

One middle-school teacher who refused to yield to "shoulds" describes her search for solutions this way:

> Neil was coming late to my fifth-period class every day. After issuing several warnings, I started keeping him after class for one minute each time he was late. But this had no effect. His next class was right down the hall and he had plenty of time to get there. He didn't have many friends and didn't socialize much between classes. In fact he seemed happy not to be part of the big rush in the halls.
>
> So I tried positive reinforcement. I told Neil that if he came to class on time each day for a week, I'd give him a coupon for a burger and fries. It turned out that he had a weekend job mowing lawns. He had money to spend

and clearly valued coming late more than a free lunch.

Then I called his parents and asked them to encourage Neil to come to class on time. It was clear he needed more motivation than that, because he still came late. I asked for a meeting with Neil and his parents, and we set up an individualized behavior plan. Under this plan I would call each day and leave a message about his behavior on their home answering machine. We set up a system of special privileges that his parents would grant or withdraw depending on whether or not he came to class on time.

This didn't work either, so I scheduled a meeting with Neil alone to discuss the problem. It came out that he had lunch fourth period, and he had been beaten up once by two other boys on his way from the cafeteria to my class. He had taken to hiding until the bell rang for fear of being waylaid again, and that was the reason for his chronic lateness.

> *I scheduled a meeting with Neil alone to discuss the issues.*

I knew better than to press Neil to reveal the names of the two boys. Instead I recruited another student—a well-respected eighth-grader—to walk with him from the cafeteria to my class for several days and to immediately report any trouble that might occur. There was no trouble. Several days of walking freely through the halls convinced Neil that he was not in danger, and he resumed coming to class on time.

The incident taught me never to second-guess the issues behind my students' behavior. I discovered that it could be critical to meet with them alone and find out what those issues are.

High-performing teachers continually seek new answers.

High-performing teachers know they don't have all the answers. But they understand that to be successful, to reach their goals and live their mission, they must continually seek new answers. They have a variety of sources for these answers:

- **Other teachers.** Colleagues are a great resource for ideas.

- **District and staff support people.** These persons can be "clearinghouses" for ideas that have worked for other teachers.

- **Professional literature.** You may find a book or a recent article that focuses on the challenge you're facing.

- **Courses and seminars.** A college or professional organization may provide valuable insights on up-to-date solutions.

"One year my entire third-grade class seemed to develop math anxiety at once," an experienced teacher recalled at a conference:

Actually it was only eight or ten kids, but they just didn't seem to "get" multiplication. None of my standard methods seemed to work. A few of this group dutifully memorized their times tables, but as for problem solving, forget it. As far as their understanding of what multiplication was, I might as well have been teaching them in Sanskrit. The other kids were leaving them behind, and I was determined not to let that happen. I tried having some of the kids who "got it" work with them, but that wasn't successful either. Then I went back to square one and tried to teach the concept all over again, but that only frustrated the children—and me.

I talked about my problem with another third-grade teacher, and she suggested that I try manipulatives. This was some time ago; manipulatives weren't exactly new, but I didn't know much about using them. They'd always struck me as the toy department, and math to me was serious business.

My colleague showed me a few of her "toys" and how she used them. She took me to a teacher-supply store where there was a greater variety. The next day she let me borrow one of her kits and try it out. My students seemed more motivated, but I felt uncomfortable. I realized that I really didn't know how to teach with manipulatives. On Saturday I went back to the school-supply store and picked up a few books on manipulatives. I also purchased some materials.

It may have been the best investment I ever made, professionally speaking. With these colorful "hands-on" tools to move around, most of the children who'd been having trouble were able to grasp the concept of multiplication readily and learn how to apply it abstractly. As for myself, manipulatives became a vital part of my tool box and I became more open in general to innovative teaching methods. When computers came in, I was the first teacher in our school to learn LOGO.

> *I talked about my problem with another third-grade teacher.*

Be a Risk Taker!

There are answers out there—and in many cases you will get the results you want just by persevering. At other times, however, positive results may elude you despite your efforts. It's at times such as these that you need to take risks.

Any time you consciously accept change, you're taking a risk. That's why most people are afraid of change. That's why most of us stay in our "comfort zones," within boundaries we know. Any change involves the risk of failure. You know that you may put a lot of effort into trying something new and find that it doesn't work. You're

Any change involves the risk of failure.

frustrated now, but you're afraid that if you strike off into unknown territory and then strike out, you're going to feel even worse. You're going to feel like a failure.

The trick is not to personalize your setbacks. Don't pin your self-esteem to your outcomes. Instead, follow the example of Thomas Edison, who is said to have quipped after many unsuccessful attempts to create a working light bulb, "I haven't failed, I found a thousand ways not to make a light bulb." As long as you can go home every day knowing you have done everything possible that day to fulfill your mission, don't regard yourself as having failed. You tried something; it didn't work; you'll try something else tomorrow.

Risk taking may involve using a new curriculum or teaching technique. If you're used to teaching math through traditional methods, using manipulatives may constitute a risk. But if there's a chance it will help students master multiplication, the high-performing teacher will take that risk.

If your comfort zone requires an orderly, controlled classroom, cooperative learning may seem risky to you. But if you're frustrated because learning isn't taking place in your orderly, controlled classroom, why not risk trying a less structured environment?

If your usual methods of classroom management don't work with a particular student, you may be taking a risk by creating an individualized behavior plan for her. But what have you got to lose? What you're doing now isn't working, is it? One former teacher, now an educational counselor, tells how she risked failure in developing such a plan for a troublesome second-grader:

Kevin couldn't keep his hands to himself. Every day, practically every hour, some other child was complaining about him poking, tugging hair, or doing something to distract them.

I tried the usual A, B, C and D. I spoke to Kevin about appropriate behavior. I took away privileges; I spoke to his parents. Nothing worked. I tried positive reinforcement—I spoke with him privately and told him that if he kept his hands to himself all day, I would reward him. That didn't work either. Behaving appropriately all day was too much for Kevin to handle at this point.

I knew he wasn't a malicious kid; he just didn't have control over his behavior. I decided he needed a coach, a personal trainer, to keep him focused on what he had to do. I knew he liked football, so the next time we talked I told him that he was going to be a football star and I was going to be his coach. I made "touchdown tickets" out of yellow tagboard and told

I gave him plenty of praise and encouragement.

Kevin that for every fifteen minutes that he kept his hands to himself, he'd earn a touchdown. We set up a scoreboard on his desk with a picture of a goal post where he could record his touchdowns. I also talked to him about what he could do in situations when he was close to other children to make sure he would be able to control his behavior.

The system really clicked with Kevin. Fifteen minutes was a reasonable time for him to be focused, and with a lot of coaching from me he got through the first few days pretty successfully. I gave him plenty of praise and encouragement, sent positive notes home to his parents, and let him trade in his tickets for special privileges at the end of the day. By the end of the first week, I was able to extend the intervals to thirty minutes, but I remained consistent with my coaching and encouragement. He continued to make progress, and his interactions with his peers were becoming much more positive.

I realize that I put in a lot of time and effort into solving this problem.

After a few more weeks, Kevin's problem had practically disappeared. We held an after-school "all-star" celebration to officially discontinue the reinforcement schedule. He was very proud.

I realize that I put in a lot of time and effort into solving this problem, but I would have had to put in just as much time coping with it—and Kevin, his classmates and I would all have been a lot worse off.

Giving a student individual attention, as in this example, always involves a double risk. Besides risking that the problem might not be solved, you also risk perceived personal rejection. But when a challenge involves an individual student, finding a way to reach him as an individual is often the only effective way to meet the challenge. A veteran of Boston-area schools told me recently, "One of the toughest problems I've ever had to face as a teacher was the violent and verbally abusive behavior of a tenth-grade boy":

Doug came from a home where violence and substance abuse were the norm. He was an angry kid who didn't care about anyone, not even himself. From the minute he entered my classroom until the bell rang, he was on a warpath. He thought nothing of yelling obscenities at me or his classmates in the middle of a lesson.

The idea of making any headway with this kid seemed impossible. But I knew if I didn't do something to solve this problem, my classroom would be in a turmoil all year, and the biggest loser would be Doug.

I set up a once-a-week fifteen-minute meeting with Doug. I told him it wasn't for punishment, but it was mandatory, and he had to come in even if he had nothing to say. The first few weeks he did nothing but complain about his other teachers and "this dumb school." I just let him talk until his time was up. The fourth week he said he didn't want to do this any more. I suggested that the following week, instead of talking, we go to the gym and play one-on-one basketball.

He agreed. When we played, he realized he could quite handily beat me at basketball, and I think he liked that. He seemed to be releasing a lot of aggression on the court. He was good, and when we finished I complimented him on his athletic ability.

After a while he began to open up to me.

We continued playing once a week after school for about forty-five minutes. After a while he began to open up to me. He told me about the verbal abuse and neglect he was subjected to at home and about the pressures he faced from peers and gang members in his neighborhood. I listened. And I told him he was a smart kid who could be anything he wanted to be if he wanted it badly enough—even a pro basketball player.

All he said was, "Yeah, right, man." But the following week he asked me, "Do you have to play college basketball before you can go pro?"

This was the beginning of his interest in college and in getting the grades he would need to get in. My problem was solved—he stopped being abusive to me—but I had no idea whether my effort had done anything for his problem until eight years later.

I was still teaching at the same school. I was sitting at

my desk grading papers after school and Doug walked into my classroom with a baby in his arms. He was twenty-three years old. He had gone to college, was married to a wonderful woman and was working as a fitness instructor at a YMCA. I wondered if he had come to blame me for setting him up for an impossible dream of playing pro basketball. But what he told me was that he wanted me to know the part I'd played in his success. "The time you spent with me that year really made a difference," he said. "You were the only adult who didn't give up on me."

You can't base your feeling of success on final outcomes.

Of course not all your efforts will be successful. No matter what risks you take, some students will not learn, some students will not behave, some methods will not work. There are no guarantees, especially with the challenges we face today. But once again: *You can't base your personal worth, your self-esteem, your feeling of success, on final outcomes.* They are not entirely within your control—as this high-school English teacher learned:

One student that, regrettably, I "lost" was a girl named Tina who was in my tenth-grade class some years ago. Tina was an average student, less mature than her peers, but a pleasant and engaging child. Then inexplicably she began balking at doing her work. She wouldn't turn in papers, and she stopped participating in discussions of the literature we read. On one test she did all right on the content-based multiple-choice questions, but she answered the interpretive questions with short, unresponsive sentences or left them blank.

I requested a personal conference with Tina and asked her whether there was anything wrong. She insisted that there was no problem, but just before she left she stated, "You should listen to people who have different opinions than you." This surprised me, as I thought I encouraged everyone to speak his or her mind in class. I told Tina that she should feel free to say or write anything she wanted, as long as it was appropriate to the subject we were discussing. She said, "Oh, sure, but you'll only give the good grades to people who agree with you!" At this point she pulled from her book bag a copy of To Kill a Mockingbird, which we had just begun to read as a class. She said, "My father says you shouldn't be teaching us this stuff, and I don't have to do any of the work if I don't want to"—and she ran out.

I wanted to find out what the problem was before it went any further. I called Tina's father that evening to see if I could set up a conference. "I'm not going to talk to you," he said when I identified myself. When I pressed him about his daughter's behavior, he called me a "Communist" and said I had "no business teaching in the schools." It turned out he had raised a fit with Tina about something I had assigned earlier—I think it was Steinbeck's The Pearl—and ever since then he'd been talking against me to her. I tried once again to get him to come in and talk to me, but he just threw more abuse at me and hung up the phone.

I didn't know anything about Tina's home life—from what I could learn her father was raising her alone—and I didn't know how I could reach her. I tried every way I could to draw her out and reassure her that her views were welcome. I even asked her if she would lead the discussion. I got no response. A week later I learned that her father had requested a transfer for her to another English class.

> *I tried every way I could to draw her out.*

Well, I knew I was OK. I didn't believe I was putting any slant on curriculum or class discussions, and I certainly wasn't grading on a "leftward political curve." No student or parent had ever accused me of anything like that. I felt badly that my efforts to reach Tina hadn't worked out, but I knew it wasn't anything I could control. I hope Tina's landed on her feet, wherever she is.

You can't personalize disappointing results. You can't consider that you've failed based on the final outcome. All you can assess your success or failure on are the responses you make.

Think about those responses now. Go back and look at your list of challenges on page 55. Get a pen and fill them in on the worksheet on the next page. Then identify possible sources for ideas that might help you overcome each challenge—other teachers, support people, books and articles, courses and seminars. Spend a little time on your research. Then go back and complete the chart by filling in a few possible responses for each challenge.

In closing this chapter, consider the words of Winston Churchill during the Battle of Britain. Here was a person who was facing many challenges, the leader of a country that was facing many challenges. And what he said to the British people is most relevant to you as a teacher: "We will never surrender."

If you know that you have not surrendered to the challenge, that you have tried everything possible, that you have searched for every answer available, you will have the satisfaction of knowing you are living your mission.

Challenge	Sources for Ideas	Possible Responses

The Power of Reaching Out to Students

Effective teachers put a priority on building positive personal relationships with their students. They recognize that such relationships are essential for day-to-day learning as well as for problem solving. But to build a positive relationship requires a student's trust. And let's face it; there is a real trust deficit out there. There are a lot of students who don't trust teachers. They don't respect teachers. They don't like teachers.

To be sure, some students do bring trust and respect into your classroom. They believe you have their best interests at heart and therefore they willingly cooperate, do what you ask of them and are motivated to succeed. But these generally are not the students who pose the challenges. And the number of students with a deep distrust of teachers is growing every year. That's why it's so tough to establish positive relationships with students today.

Some teachers approach this trust deficit by rationalizing why it shouldn't apply to them: "I give so much to my students—my time, my attention, my knowledge. They should trust me." But by now you know where such thinking leads.

Trust Line ⎯⎯⎯⎯⎯⎯⎯⎯⎯⎯⎯⎯⎯⎯⎯⎯⎯⎯⎯⎯⎯⎯⎯⎯⎯⎯⎯⎯⎯⎯⎯⎯⎯⎯⎯⎯⎯⎯⎯

Secondary School
Involved in School Activities

Good Relationships with Peers

Middle School
Continued Parent Involvement

Teacher Encouragement

Good Grades

Elementary School
Parental Motivation and Guidance

Gets Along with Teacher and Students

STUDENT A
Begins Kindergarten with Positive Support from Parents

STUDENT B
Begins Kindergarten: Negative Parent Attitude Toward School

Behavior Problems in Elementary School

Elementary School
Lack of Motivation

Doesn't Get Along with Peers

Defiant Behavior Toward Teachers

Middle School
Detention

Increased Negativity from Teachers

Poor Grades

Secondary School
Suspensions

The fact is that every one of your students has established a positive or negative level of trust in you *before he or she even reaches your classroom.* The process begins before the first day of kindergarten, depending on whether or not parents communicate respect for school and teachers. It develops further as the student accumulates experiences with school. As a result, through no fault of your own, many students enter your classroom with the attitude that you're not on their side.

High-performing teachers have made a paradigm shift that empowers them to reach such students. Pay close attention: Instead of seeing your relationship with students in terms of what you give to *them*, you need to recognize that to do your job you need to have them give something to you. You need them to give you their attention, their cooperation, their respect—their trust.

"If more kids had someone they could trust, and talk to, many kids could really be changed," asserts one award-winning teacher. Indeed, it's a basic law of human relations. The more we trust, respect, care

> *The question is, of course, how do you build that trust?*

about a person, the more we're willing to give of ourselves to that person. The more your students are willing to give to you, the closer you are to fulfilling your mission.

The question, of course, is how do you build that trust? "It'd be nice to just get up there and teach, the way it is in college," another teacher comments, "but that's not the way it works. I mean, these kids are fighting you. They don't believe that you are really there for them. How can they believe it if they don't trust you? And the only way they can trust you is when you get to know them and they can feel that you care about them."

It's as though you had a unique emotional bank account with each student. With some students you start off with a high, positive balance. These are the students who arrive in your classroom willing and ready to learn. With others your balance is close to zero or perhaps even negative.

Now, the point to remember is this: Any time you ask a student to give you respect, attention or cooperation, you make a withdrawal from your account with that student. With some students you can make withdrawals for weeks without depleting the account. With others, you overdraw your balance in one day. As for those with whom you start off in the red, they're going to challenge you the first time you ask anything of them.

You can't accomplish anything without trust. Your priority, therefore, is to make deposits into your students' trust accounts. You must work constantly to build them up by reaching out to students—by letting them know you care.

> *The high-performing teacher actively*
> *reaches out to students in order to*
> *build their trust.*

Six Strategies for Building a Positive Balance of Trust

How do you go about building your students' trust? The first thing to recognize is that you won't get very far trying to reach out to them only as students. You need to relate to them as people, as one human being to another.

This does not mean taking a generic, tell-me-how-you're-feeling-today approach. Students will quickly spot this as empty and insincere. Nor does it mean trying to become their friend. As one experienced teacher puts it, "If you try to come on as their buddy, they'll eat you for breakfast." Be friendly, certainly, but never forget that you're their teacher.

Apart from avoiding these pitfalls, there are a number of strategies you can use to build trust in your students:

1. Treat students as you would want your own child to be treated.

Every student deserves to be treated with respect and caring. If you're unsure of what this means, think of how you would want your own child to be treated by his or her teacher. "My son had a problem with a teacher when he was in the second grade," one of our associates relates:

> Ron was having a lot of trouble with his penmanship, and this teacher had absolutely no patience with him. He used to come home in tears because of the way she'd ridicule him in front of the class. It made me think carefully about how I related to my own students. I made an effort never to "get in their face." I made a conscious effort never to say or do anything that would diminish a student's self-esteem. I have succeeded in making such an attitude part of my teaching style so that I no longer consciously do it, but from time to time I do still stop and ask myself, "Is this the way I'd like a teacher to relate to my children?"

2. Get to know your students.

Developing personal relationships means taking the time to know your students. You aren't just teaching spelling, earth science, long division. You aren't just teaching a class of thirty-five students. You're teaching thirty-five individual young human beings.

Discover your students' likes, dislikes, interests, and hobbies. Find out what experiences have shaped their attitudes toward school. Gain insights into the challenges they face outside of your classroom. Identify those who need extra attention, firmer limits, extra motivation. By taking the time to learn and apply such information, you'll reveal yourself to your students as a person who cares about them.

Discover your students' likes, dislikes, interests and hobbies.

Student Interest Inventory

Name _____

Adults who live with me:

Name _____

Name _____

Name _____

Name _____

Brothers and Sisters:

Name _____ Age _____

Name _____ Age _____

Name _____ Age _____

Name _____ Age _____

Special friends: _____

_____

What I like to do most at home: _____

_____

These are my favorite hobbies: _____

_____

This is my favorite book: _____

This is my favorite TV show: _____

This is my favorite movie: _____

If I had one wish, I would want to: _____

_____

School would be better if: _____

_____

If I had a million dollars, I would: _____

_____

This is what my teacher did last year that I liked the most: _____

_____

This is what my teacher did last year that I liked the least: _____

_____

One way to get to know students as unique individuals is to use student interest inventories, like the sample on the facing page. Modify the form if necessary to make it appropriate to your students. Pay particular attention to responses to open-ended questions such as those at the bottom of the sample. They can be very revealing, as in these examples from fourth-grade children:

- "If I had one wish, I would want my dad to come back home."

- "If I had one wish, I would want my sister to not be sick."

- "School would be better if there were no drugs, gangs and guns."

- "This is what my teacher did last year that I liked the least: She tore up my paper in front of the whole class."

Another technique is to have students create personal journals. They may surprise you with their openness, especially if you write back to them. "My fifth-grade students have really opened up to me through their personal journals, one of our associates reports. "They've shared such concerns as these:

My fifth-grade students have really opened up to me.

- 'My mom smokes pot in front of me. What can I do?'

- 'All the kids hate me and they won't play with me because I'm fat.'

- 'It's been three days since my dog ran away. Sometimes when I'm sitting at my desk, I think I hear her barking. I think maybe she's out in front of the school waiting for me. But when school's out, she's never there. Do you think she'll ever come back?'

- 'There are these three dudes I hang with [sic]. They've been stealing things out of the deli and they think I'm a wuss because I won't do it. I know stealing is wrong, but I hate it when they make fun of me.'

3. Listen to your students.

Many students aren't used to having a teacher (or any adult) willing to spend time listening to their concerns.

Think about growing up without any adult to talk to.

Think about this a moment. Think about growing up without any adult to talk to. If you have a student living under such circumstances, and you spend some time listening to her, you'll be making a large deposit to her trust account.

"I had this defiant, angry seventh-grader, Jillian, who gave me a lot of backtalk and profanity," reports an Ohio teacher:

On one occasion she provoked a confrontation in which her vocabulary reduced itself to two words—you can guess which two. I defused the confrontation and met with Jillian after class. She started mouthing off to me again: "Nobody understands me." "You're on my case." "School sucks." Instead of responding as she expected—"Don't speak to me like that, young lady"; "You've got a bad attitude"—I chose to listen nonjudgmentally as she put down teachers, the principal, her parents, other kids at school. I listened—but I also stated my expectations for her behavior in my classroom.

The next day wasn't any better. I met with her again after school and let her vent more steam. I learned that Jillian's father was an alcoholic who had disappeared when she was eight. Her mother was on crack. There was often no food in the house. No one was cooking meals or doing laundry. "I have this brother who's nine," Jillian told me. "No one's taking care of him or seeing that he's safe."

Listening to her I became aware of certain things—why her way of thinking and behaving made sense to her, why she didn't see any point in schoolwork or achievement, why you have to listen to students like Jillian in order to understand them. During our third one-to-one, I could tell that having an adult there to listen was filling a deep and painful void. She stopped verbally abusing me. She still didn't do much work, but she discontinued her open hostility in class.

I told Jillian I'd be there for her any time she wanted to talk. I told her that I thought a lot of her, that I cared, that I believed in her ability to overcome the challenges she faced. I wished it would have been appropriate for me to tell her to redirect her anger at her parents' dysfunctional lifestyle but I had to settle for telling her that she didn't have to be limited by it.

Soon afterward, she began seeking me out to talk.

4. Develop empathy.

When Jillian's teacher put herself in her student's shoes, she discovered that there were reasons for the girl's anger, and her distrust of the adult world. By developing such empathy for your students, you can go a long way toward winning their trust. Instead of simply reacting to their inappropriate behavior, try to understand where they're coming from.

Try to understand where they're coming from.

The child who curses you may have had only negative experiences with adults. The child who daydreams in class and can't seem to concentrate may be the object of a bitter custody fight between his parents. The child who reacts to every criticism with a threat of violence may live in environment where all confrontations are settled by violence. The child who is sullen and uncommunicative may have spent the last night on the street.

"I had a student, a fourth-grade girl, who was extremely withdrawn," reports one teacher:

> She didn't participate in class, didn't do her homework and rarely completed classwork. On the playground she seemed to prefer playing by herself to mixing with other children.
>
> It turned out that her mother was pressing charges against the child's uncle for having sexually abused her two years ago. The girl was in therapy and was also being prepared to testify in court. When I learned this, I realized that it would it be inappropriate to try to address her behavior. I imagined how my own daughter might react under such circumstances. I felt that the best approach to take with this child was to allow her space and let her heal, and to let her know that I'm here for her.

Empathy does not mean making excuses for the student. It does mean recognizing that a student's negative behavior may not itself be the problem—it may be an expression of his or her need. The more empathy you develop, the more trust you will build—and the more your students will give you what you need to be successful.

The more empathy you develop, the more trust you will build.

5. Recognize the challenges your students face.

Many students face enormous challenges. Poverty, family breakups, lack of adult concern can all chip away at a student's self-esteem. Be aware of the impact you can have. The smile, the thumbs up, the caring words you share with a student may be the only positive feedback she receives from an adult all day.

In some cases, as in the last example, personal space and the knowledge that you care may be all the feedback you can give—and all you need to build the student's trust. In others you can take a more active role. A high-school English teacher relates how her awareness of the challenges faced by one of her students led her to reach out to him:

> When Dario was in my class his senior year, he was unreceptive to anything I tried to help him with. In the middle of that year he dropped out of school, but he came back the next fall as a fifth-year senior. During his time away from school, he had been totally on his own. He had been living with his grandmother, but she had died. He had moved in with a friend, another boy, and had gotten in some minor trouble with the police. Dario was afraid. He realized that unless he finished school, he didn't have much of a future.
>
> Other teachers were skeptical of his sincerity or his resolve. He'd been a troublesome, difficult student, and it was understandable that they doubted him. But I really liked Dario, and I wanted to make this work out for him.
>
> I arranged for him to go to the middle school that fed our high school and talk to at-risk kids. I asked him to speak to them about the value of

He knew I believed in him.

> staying in school, working hard and believing in themselves. It helped to have others who looked up to him, but what he was really doing was talking himself into believing what he was saying. He needed to experience a degree of success to believe in himself. I worked individually with Dario on his academics before and after school. I gave him extra help and extra assignments. He knew I believed in him, and he had some friends in the class who encouraged him as well. I urged them to keep encouraging him, and that really helped. It was important

for Dario to know that he had people in his life that really cared.

He graduated—barely, but he did it.

He joined the Navy. He came back to visit the week before he went in. He was very excited. He'd had a full-time job all that summer. He was feeling good about himself and was hopeful about what his future might bring.

6. Discuss nonacademic issues.

One of the most effective ways to demonstrate empathy with your students is by sharing conversations unrelated to academics. Talk to them about issues of interest to them—their triumphs and concerns, their problems and achievements. Use your knowledge of them to guide you in initiating such conversations. If you know that a student plays in a Saturday soccer league, for example, ask her on Monday how her game went.

I made a point to ask him about this interest of his.

If you know that a student has been clashing with his boss at his after-school job, ask him how things are going—and praise him for sticking out the difficult situation.

If you know that a student enjoys a TV show you watch regularly, initiate a conversation with her about the latest episode.

If you know that your student has a particular hobby, interest or passion, encourage him to share his enthusiasm with you. "Jerry was always disrupting the class by talking to himself and making noises," said one sixth-grade teacher:

> When I spoke to him, I found out that he was interested in ventriloquism. The noises he was making were his "practice." I told him that my class was not an appropriate place for him to practice ventriloquism, but I also made a point over the next few days to ask him about this interest of his. I let him make a dummy as an art project,

and once I set aside fifteen minutes for him to perform for the class. By then Jerry was no longer disrupting the class, and I was finding him much more responsive to assignments.

Six More Techniques for Building Relationships with Students

By reaching out to students, by learning about them as individuals, by listening to them and being empathetic to their needs, you lay a solid foundation for building that trust. Now let's explore a few ways in which you can build on that foundation—some quick ideas we've learned from high-performing teachers:

1. Use student interest inventories.

Use a survey like the one on page 76 early in the year. Your students may or may not choose to reveal the more private aspects of their lives, but at the very least you can discover the many personal interests they have: ballet, baseball, basketball, roller blading, soccer, coin collecting, comic-book collecting, stuffed-animal collecting, cats, dogs, horses, volcanoes, word games,

> *Use students' interests as conversation starters during one-to-one time.*

ancient civilizations, guitar, saxophone, cooking, photography, motorcycles, movie special effects, wildlife preservation—the list is endless. Use students' interests as conversation starters during one-to-one time. Integrate them into your lesson plans and class discussions. Work them into suggested topics for book reports, science projects or writing activities. By letting a student know you find his interests worth talking about, you raise his self-esteem—and build his trust.

2. Spend one-to-one time.

Don't wait until a problem develops to get to know your students individually. Be proactive. Let students know you're interested by asking them to meet with you for a private talk. It can be an opportunity for you both to communicate in a nonthreatening context. Yes, your time is valuable, but meeting alone with students to discuss their interests and concerns (not their classwork or behavior) will pay trust dividends. And if you absolutely cannot spare any after-school time this week, try walking around the classroom and talking to students while they're engaged in independent work—not about their work, but about them.

3. Call a student after a bad day.

We all have bad days with students. You send a powerful message of concern when you pick up the phone after school, call the student and say, "You and I had a pretty bad day today. I feel bad about it. What can we do to have a better day tomorrow?"

What can we do to have a better day tomorrow?

Sometimes students will resist your approach, especially if there's been an on-going negative relationship between you. That's all the more reason to persist, as in this conversation reported by a former teacher. One of his sixth-graders had been a frequent discipline problem during the first month of school. On this occasion the boy had gotten up during a math lesson for a drink of water and then spit it out on the back of another boy's neck. The teacher had "lost it" and ordered him to the principal's office.

Teacher: Brad, you and I had a bad day today. What happened was upsetting to both of us.

Student: Yeah, because of you I got detention. How's it your business bothering me at home?

Teacher: Brad, we've got the whole school year ahead of us, and I know it can be a good one, but it's got to be both of us together. Let's start by talking about what we can do to make tomorrow a better day.

Student: You can start by getting off my case.

Teacher: I'll get off your case, Brad. I'll treat you with the same respect as I treat every other student. That's something I can do. Now, what can you do?

Student: I don't have to do anything.

Teacher: You're right. Nobody has to do anything. You have control over yourself. You choose the way you want things to be. What could you choose for yourself that will make it a better day for you tomorrow?

Student: I don't know. I guess I won't spit water on anyone.

Teacher: Good. Anything else?

Student: Uhhhh... (with a sigh) I'll stay in my seat and pay attention. But math is totally boring.

Teacher: Not spitting water, staying in your seat and paying attention will be a great start. And if math gets so boring that you just can't take it any more, you can give me some kind of a quiet signal and I'll see what I can do. Deal?

Student: I guess.

Teacher: Thanks, Brad. I really want this to work out for us. I care about you, and I want you to know that I'm here for you this year no matter what. I'll see you tomorrow.

4. Call a student when he or she is sick.

Asking after someone's health is something that caring people do. When you call a student and say, "Hello, how are you feeling? I've missed you this week," you let her (and her parents) know that you are thinking of her, that you see her as a worthwhile individual.

5. Attend student events.

Students of all grade levels are proud of their participation in sports, musical and dramatic performances, and other activities. When you cheer a student at a basketball game (and recap the game with him afterward), when you go up to a student after a play and tell her how much you enjoyed her performance, you make him or her feel prouder still. Your attendance at such events emphasizes your interest in them as people, not just as students.

6. Write positive notes.

You might be amazed at the trust and respect that results.

Get into the habit of jotting down a few kind words to your students when something positive is on your mind. Yes, it takes some time, but don't you take the time to communicate with your students when something negative needs addressing? You might be amazed at the trust and respect that results when a student receives a note such as this:

Dear Lanie,

The story you told today couldn't have been more appropriate. You are very smart to see the similarities between your story and the one we were reading. Best of all was the way you told it. I saw some students on the verge of tears. You really added something to my lesson I never could have planned on my own. Thank you, Lanie. I'm very impressed.

Above all, do not take your relationships with your students for granted. Never forget that success with students depends on your winning and keeping their trust—and that a trusting relationship requires nurturing and attention.

When you make that paradigm shift, when you recognize that there are students coming into your classroom without a lot of trust to give, you become tremendously empowered. You know things aren't the way they "should" be—but you know too that by reaching out to your students, you can build relationships that will make them caring and cooperative human beings. You can go home every day with the satisfaction that you've made a difference.

You can live your mission.

The Power of Reaching Out to Parents

If you ever wonder *why* you have to deal with so many challenges in the classroom, here's something to think about: What motivated *you* to do your work when you were in school? Why did you pay attention to your teachers? Why did you behave?

I'll tell you why *I* behaved in school. There were two key reasons. Number one was my mom. Number two was my dad.

So it is with most successful students. Parents are the most influential people in a child's life. No one else has such power to motivate or guide a child. No one else has such power to communicate the importance of education.

And *there* is the problem. In the past teachers could usually count on receiving parents' support. Today they cannot. They reveal their frustration in such statements as:

- "I feel alone in my classroom. It shouldn't be like this."

- "I can't get anywhere with these kids when their parents treat me like the enemy."

- "My students come into class hungry and exhausted. How are they supposed to learn?"

- "If their parents don't teach them how to behave, what chance have I got?"

- "I don't know how to begin to work with parents."

You know you need the support of parents. The trouble may be that you are trying to enlist their support through traditional means, based on traditional assumptions about the teacher-parent partnership. Chances are you set aside time to meet them only once a year at back-to-school night, or twice a year at conferences. Otherwise you contact them only when a problem arises.

In many cases these responses no longer work. There are parents today who don't trust teachers. There are parents who don't respect school. There are parents who are so overwhelmed with the pressures of their own lives that they don't know what they can do to help their children succeed.

Parental support is absolutely critical to the success of their mission.

High-performing teachers recognize that parental support is absolutely critical to the success of their mission. They therefore make a paradigm shift that empowers them to work effectively with parents who may feel negative or helpless. These teachers shift responsibility for parent involvement from the *parents* to *themselves*. They *take the initiative* for opening and maintaining channels of communication with parents. They see this as one of their key responsibilities.

Because this initiative involves risk of failure and a commitment of time, you may be reluctant to take it. But once you have made the effort, you will realize how much easier it makes your job.

I've seen it happen time and time again. As one teacher puts it, "There are two reasons why I establish a relationship with parents. One is for the sake of the child, because many of these kids I cannot turn around alone. The second reason is selfish. When parents are involved, problems often go away and my life as a teacher is much easier."

> *The high-performing teacher takes*
> *proactive steps to build positive*
> *relationships with parents.*

The Golden Rule of Parent Involvement

It's important to recognize that in spite of the responses you receive, most parents *are* concerned when their children have problems in school. They *want* to help their children do better. Most of the time they just don't know what to do. Studies have shown that parents will respond positively if you approach them positively. As one teacher explains it, "I have learned that parents are there most of the time for us if we know how to communicate with them, and if they know how much we care about their children."

There's one key rule that will enable you to gain and keep the support of most parents. I call it the Golden Rule of Parent Involvement: *Treat parents as you would want your child's teacher to treat you.*

Many parents today are hostile or indifferent to teachers because they have negative memories of their own school experiences. It follows that if all they hear from you about their child is negative, it pushes their own negative buttons. If they perceive that you are "talking down" to them or are not interested in what they have to say, they may feel that you aren't sincere in asking for their involvement. If their only contact with you is at a midyear conference or back-to-school night, they may conclude that you don't care. It's crucial to present yourself to parents as a caring and concerned professional—by being conscious of how you would like *your* child's teacher to treat *you.*

How would *you* want to be spoken to?

How would *you* want to be listened to?

If there was a problem, would you want the teacher to help you with it?

Would you want to hear only about problems, or would you also want to hear from the teacher when your child was doing well?

If your child developed a learning or behavior problem, would you prefer to hear about it at once, or only after it had gotten out of hand? Would you rather hear it expressed as a concern about the child or as a burden on the teacher?

"I was doing it all wrong," one teacher recalls about her early years in the classroom:

> I had no training in dealing with parents. I had this attitude that you couldn't reach them; you couldn't approach them, and even if you tried they wouldn't know what to do. It was *my* attitude, but I was projecting it onto them. So when I'd call a parent, it would only be if I couldn't do anything with the child, and I'd say something like, "Your child is driving me nuts; what are you going to do about it?" And of course they'd get defensive. They'd say something like, "Don't ask me, lady; he drives me nuts too." Or they'd say, "You're the teacher. Do your job." And I'd tell myself, "See? There's no talking to these people."

> *I had no training in dealing with parents.*

> It was after my own son started school that I questioned my approach. Adam was reading when he was three, but he'd always had trouble with coordination. So when his teacher told me in effect that he was "slow" because he couldn't draw a house and had trouble buttoning his jacket, it infuriated me. I decided that she didn't know what she was doing. But after I cooled off, it occurred to me that many parents over the years must have had the same reaction to me.

> I asked myself just what it was that bothered me about

this teacher's message. I analyzed what I was doing in my approaches to parents. I'd been undiplomatic, unspecific, unhelpful. After I got past the *mea culpa* stage, I sat down and wrote out some ideas about what I could do differently.

For one thing, I could *establish contact with parents before any problems came up.* I realized I could have heard Adam's teacher's negative comments with a lot less hostility if she'd ever taken the trouble to contact me when there was something good to report.

> *I could let them know I cared about their child.*

Another thing I could do was *call about a problem* before *it reached the driving-me-nuts stage.* I could plan what I was going to say before I called. I could tell the parents exactly what the problem was. I could tell them what I had already done about the problem and what other things I might do. I could give them specific ideas about how *they* might help me. But most of all, I could let them know I cared about their child.

Once I started putting these ideas into effect, it was amazing how approachable, how *helpful,* most parents became.

Parents *can* be helpful—if they think you're there to help *them.* Don't anticipate an adversarial relationship, or you may be creating one. You're talking about their children—the most important people in their lives. And so you must be sensitive to their feelings, especially when you talk to them about a problem. Be aware of the pain they might be feeling about that very problem.

Teacher: Mr. Reynolds, I'm glad you were able to find the time to meet with me. I'm concerned about Jenessa's progress in reading. She's really trying, but she has a lot of difficulty with anything above a second-grade level. I've sent several notes home with her asking you to read with her for fifteen to twenty minutes each evening.

Parent: I know. I know Jenessa is way behind in reading. We feel terrible about it, and we want to help her, but we just don't have the time to read with her at night.

Teacher: I know how hectic evenings can be with all the responsibilities you must have, but . . .

Parent: Look, my wife and I both work. By the time we get home and get dinner on the table, feed and bathe the baby, get some chores done, return phone calls and help Jenessa with her regular homework, it's time for her to go to bed. Some nights she has soccer practice, and I'm taking a class two nights a week. It's not like we're just sitting around watching TV.

Teacher: I understand. You're caring parents and you want the best for Jenessa. So do I. I have some ideas about how we can work together to help her improve her reading. I've arranged for my instructional aide to work with Jenessa and

I have some ideas about how we can work together.

two other students who are having similar problems. I've given the aide training in this kind of work, and she'll be monitoring their progress. I'll also be structuring a lot of partner work for Jenessa. She seems to respond well to it. I'll team her up with a more advanced reader who can get her through trouble spots. In addition, I'll work with her as much as I can during our lessons and cooperative group activities. Okay?

Parent: You're the teacher.

Teacher: Now, here is what I'd like you to do. Think of your reading time with Jenessa as important as your chores or your phone calls. Each of you choose three nights a week to read with her for fifteen minutes. After the baby's asleep might be the best time. Write down the dates and times in your calendar. You may be surprised at the time you find if you plan it. Choose a quiet, cozy spot and make it an enjoyable time for you and Jenessa. You can take turns reading. Don't worry about her skills. Just read for enjoyment and, most importantly, talk about the stories.

You may be surprised at the time you find if you plan it.

Parent: What stories?

Teacher: I'll give you some books she'll enjoy and be able to read. Read one each night. If Jenessa likes one, feel free to read it again. When you've finished these, I'll give you more. If she shows an interest in another book or a magazine, let her follow her interests. The idea is to give her as much opportunity to read as possible. It will help her understanding and make her feel more comfortable about reading. How does that sound? Do you have any questions?

Parent: No. It sounds like you have a plan all worked out, and I realize we have to make some kind of commitment to a plan. One hour a week seems the least we can do.

Teacher: Great! Please call any time you have questions or problems. I'll be in touch to see how things are going. I know that by working together we can make a difference for Jen.

Of course there will be times when you *do* find yourself in an adversarial relationship with parents. But if you observe the Golden Rule, you may soon find yourself receiving their support. Put yourself on the parents' side. Initiate a dialogue, not a monologue, about measures you both can take to address the problem. Demonstrate your confidence in your ability to work with their child. Explain your ideas, but don't neglect to listen to theirs as well. If you show respect for them as concerned parents, they'll see you as a partner rather than as an adversary:

> *Initiate a dialogue, not a monologue, about measures you can take.*

Teacher: Hello, Mrs. Gelman? This is Mrs. Moreno. I'll be John's teacher this year. I called to let you know that I'm looking forward to working with your son and doing whatever I can to make this a terrific year for him.

Parent: Maybe you don't know about my son. He's been in a lot of trouble at school, and I'm sure this year won't be any different.

Teacher: I know he's been in trouble before, and I'm going to do everything I can to make this year different for him. I know you want the best for him, and so do I.

Parent: His teacher last year said the same thing, and it lasted all of two weeks. What do you figure you can do?

Teacher: Helping your son to be successful in school may not be easy and it may take some time, but I've made a commitment and I will follow through with it. Is there anything you could think of right now that would help me make this year more successful for John?

Parent: *You're* asking *me?* Well, let me tell you. The last two years he was always being sent to the office or given detention, and it didn't seem to make any difference. I'd hate to see another year go by where he's constantly kicked out of class or kept after school and the problems just keep getting worse.

Teacher: That's a good point. If those methods don't work for John, there's no reason to use them. I've had a lot of experience working with students like him, and I'm confident that together we can help him be more successful without constantly resorting to such action.

Parent: Yeah, well, good luck. My son is a handful. Nobody's been able to handle him. Most of the time I don't know what to do with him myself.

Teacher: I'm sure I'll have some ideas once I've had a chance to get to know him. I'll be in touch again once school begins. If you have any concerns before then, please don't hesitate to call. You can leave a message with the school secretary, and I'll get back to you as soon as I can. I'll stay in close communication with you this year so that John will see we're both behind him.

> *I'm confident that together we can help him be more successful.*

Four Proactive Techniques for Gaining Parents' Support

You need parents to see that their children's basic needs are met so that they come to school healthy and ready to learn. You need them to make sure their children do assigned homework. You need them to support your discipline efforts. You need them to support their children's successes with positive recognition. You need them to communicate to you any essential information that would impact their children's well-being. You need them to ask you questions when they are unsure of what to do.

In other words, you need a lot from parents.

> *You have to give parents what they need.*

To get it, you have to give parents what *they* need: positive communication, respect and the continual assurance that you're working in their children's best interests. With the "Golden Rule" as a guiding principle, let's look at a few strategies you can use to show parents that you're worthy of their support.

1. Contact parents before school begins.

If possible, introduce yourself to your students' parents before the school year begins. Send them a note letting them know that you're looking forward to working with them and their child. Communicate your hopes and expectations.

In some cases, where the child has a history of problems, you may want to phone the parents before school starts. Remember that they're probably used to hearing from teachers only when there is trouble. Give them an impression of your confident expectations and your professionalism *before* you need to enlist their help.

2. Send positive notes.

Think about how you would feel about your child's teacher if you only heard from her when something was wrong. Yet it's a fact that parents usually hear from teachers only when there's a problem.

Even the most difficult students have moments of success. Don't let those moments pass unnoticed. Phone parents or drop them notes to tell them what their child is doing right. They will be much

Even the most difficult students have moments of success.

more likely to give support when it's needed if they have received messages like this:

> Dear Ms. Brockert:
>
> Just wanted you to know what a great job Toni did on her science report. The model of the bears' den she made showed a lot of care and creativity, and the class really enjoyed her oral presentation. You should be very proud of her!

On occasions when you do have to report a problem, follow it up with a progress report. "I've found that it's imperative to communicate with parents when the child is doing well, not only when there's a problem," one teacher asserts:

There are numerous ways of establishing a relationship with parents. I think the easiest way is to call them when the child is good. Tell them when their child is showing improvement in his work and in his attitude, and congratulate them. I want them to realize that there are things we can do together to turn their son or daughter around.

3. Establish regular communication.

Parents need to know what's going on in their child's classroom, but don't expect them to find out from the child! When they ask, "What went on in school today," they usually get back one of two answers: "Nothing," or "Oh, you know, same old stuff."

Let parents know what's going on in your class—the curriculum you're covering, the assignments you've given the class, the methods you're using. Write a bulletin once or twice a month and send copies home. The more parents know about what you're doing, the more likely they are to support you. When you ask a parent why his child hasn't turned in his long-range project, he won't ask you, "What project?" When you put in a call for help, parents will have a better idea of *how* they can help—and they'll appreciate that you took the trouble to keep them informed.

4. Help parents with problems.

Most parents want to help their children; they just don't know what to do. They need answers—to academic questions, homework issues, disciplinary problems. You're a professional. Serve as a resource for parents in all aspects of their children's education. Let them know of your availability. Go out of your way to arrange a conference time to accommodate a parent's schedule. You'll find that the great majority of parents will follow your advice if you show them that you know your stuff—and that you care.

> *You're a professional. Serve as a resource for parents.*

This was the experience of a second-grade teacher who helped a child through a difficult situation by reaching out to her parents:

> Ivy had no reading or writing skills. She barely spoke. I wanted to get her into a special-education program so that she could spend part of the day in the resource room and receive the individual instruction she needed. I called her parents in to talk about a referral, but they were adamantly against the idea of putting Ivy in a special class. After I explained my concerns, showed them samples of her work and told them what I'd done so far, their attitude changed. I think they started to see that I really cared about their daughter and was doing all I could for her. I described the lengthy referral process and emphasized my concern about getting the services Ivy needed as soon as possible. By the end of the conference, they were not only supportive of the idea, they were eager to do anything they could to speed up the process.

A high-school teacher describes how she helped keep a troubled student from becoming a dropout by reaching out to his mother:

Nick was such a behavior problem that at one point he was called before the board of education. He was a junior, and he wanted to quit school. He was in one of my classes, and I knew that if there was any hope of saving him it would be through a team effort with his parents.

I arranged to meet with Nick's mom. She was beside herself. The problems he was having at school were interfering with other areas of his life. I told her that I knew about Nick's situation and would do what I could to help him. Together we brainstormed how to create some positive things in his life. I gave her some ideas on how to be more supportive toward him at home. I offered him work in the drama department working backstage on lights and special effects.

He's a senior now, and he's doing much better. He's working hard and staying involved. His mom has written me several notes thanking me for helping Nick get through that dreadful time.

It all comes down to this: The more you reach out to parents and the more you show them that you care, the more support you will get from them. If you take proactive steps to involve parents, you'll

The more you reach out, the more support you will get.

find your efforts returned tenfold when you need their help. And that help is exactly what you need to ensure your success—to make a difference with those students you care about.

Chapter 8

The Power of a Positive Attitude

To be a successful teacher, you need to focus on the positive—on your strengths, your students' capabilities, all the positive aspects of your work. If you focus on the negative instead, you compromise your ability to fulfill your mission.

There's a simple exercise that demonstrates how positive thoughts are critical to your success. Imagine this situation: You're on a mountain ledge, two feet wide and six thousand feet up. One false step and you fall to oblivion. Close your eyes for a few moments and feel yourself on that ledge in vivid detail.

Scary, wasn't it? Did you find your heart beating faster, your palms sweating? There you are, sitting comfortably reading a book, but your body reacted as though you were in mortal danger.

Now close your eyes again. This time imagine yourself in the most relaxing circumstances you can think of: a sunlit meadow, a beach in Hawaii, your bed on a Sunday morning. Place yourself there in your mind and experience what you're feeling.

Are you relaxed? That's the power of thoughts. They're not just innocent little microwatts of energy in your brain. Thoughts have a powerful impact on your mind and body. The part of your mind that controls those automatic, physical responses can't tell the difference between reality and what you are thinking. When you have negative thoughts, so research indicates, your body produces hormones that create stress, anxiety and fatigue. When your thoughts are positive, your body produces chemicals that lead to a sense of well-being, relaxation and greater energy.

Now what does this have to do with teaching? Simply this: *You have a choice* as to whether you want to focus on the positive or the negative aspects of your job, and that choice can determine how hard your job is. High-performing teachers choose to focus on their strengths, not their weaknesses. They choose to focus on their students' abilities, not their deficits. They choose to focus on solutions, not problems. And with this choice, they greatly reduce their stress level and enhance their effectiveness.

> *The high-performing teacher chooses*
> *to maintain a positive attitude*
> *in the classroom.*

Making a Case for the Positive

It's as though you had two lawyers presenting evidence in your mind. One lawyer makes a case for how hard it is to be a teacher today: "The kids aren't prepared. The parents don't care. The administration doesn't support you." The other lawyer argues for the positive side: "Teaching is rewarding. You have the chance to touch the lives of young people. You have the power to make a difference."

There's a third officer of this court—the judge. Every day you listen to both lawyers and make judicial rulings between them. There is compelling evidence on both sides, but you have the power to *choose* which evidence you are going to accept or reject. You have a choice whether to accept the positive or the negative evidence. The choice you make can determine whether you spend the day huddled on a precipice or relaxing on the beach.

"By maintaining a positive attitude you're not sapped of energy like you are when you're negative," observes one high-performing teacher. "You create a space for kids where they are enjoying themselves, and you go home feeling good about yourself."

Another teacher articulates it this way: "I keep a positive focus because I have to. It's my buoy in the ocean. It's my tool of survival."

Negative thoughts lead to negative emotions and negative behavior. The effects begin when you're on your way to work. You think about how tough things are and you anticipate the problems you are going to have. By the time you arrive, your emotions have either reached a place of anger—"Doggone it, I'm not going to take that!"—or of hopelessness—"Why am I here? What's the point?" The result? You enter the classroom looking for problems instead of successes.

Negative thoughts lead to negative behavior.

In turn your negative emotions affect your students, who send them back at you in the form of hostility or indifference. You respond by getting even more upset and discouraged—and so do they. You trap yourself and your students in a downward spiral.

Now let's look at the impact of positive thoughts. What happens if you think about students who have been making progress? What happens if you focus on lessons that have been effective recently; if you concentrate on whom you're going to help that day? With thoughts like these you come into the classroom relaxed, energized, in a good mood. *You look for success.* You reinforce your students in a positive way, and they catch your positiveness. They become relaxed and energized. They act in a positive manner and refuel your own positive attitude. You're soaring.

"I had been teaching in a school where morale was low," reports a high-school math teacher from southern California:

> Classes were too large, there were students with a wide range of abilities and special needs, there wasn't nearly enough planning time, and there had been almost yearly

cuts in services and supplies. Everyone seemed to have a negative attitude. The principal stayed in her office all day and gave us no direction. The teachers, myself included, were just going through the motions, and so were the kids. I didn't see any point in approaching it any other way—I thought I was just accepting reality.

This year I transferred to another school, and I just can't believe the difference. It has the same basic problems as my old school, but what a happier place! The teachers are so much more positive and enthusiastic, and they have a better handle on things. They have a wonderful rapport with the principal. He's a good listener; he's always willing to help solve a problem. He seems to genuinely care about the people on his staff. He knows most of the students by name and is generally visible throughout the school. The teachers seem to enjoy the work they do. They're very supportive of one another, and there's a level of cooperation with parents that wouldn't even have been a dream at my old school.

At first this felt foreign. I modeled myself after other teachers, but I was self-conscious with their behaviors and speaking patterns. After a few weeks, though, I could feel myself slipping into a whole new mode of thinking. I noticed a difference in the way I spoke to students and colleagues and a tremendous difference in the responses I got from them. All my relationships seem more productive, more rewarding, even those out of school. I feel more relaxed, yet I seem to get more work done than at my old school. Best of all, my students are having a terrific year. Achievement is high, and parents are pleased. For the first time I'm seeing how success really does breed success.

> *I could feel myself slipping into a whole new mode of thinking.*

That's the power of a positive attitude. It keeps your energy high, it keeps you motivated, and it helps you to perform at your highest level. When you're feeling positive, you focus on students who are

Your positive energy produces positive responses.

getting things right. You're lavish in your positive reinforcement. You feel more motivated to reach out to parents. Your positive energy produces positive responses, and those responses send your efforts and results rocketing upward.

A principal from suburban Kansas City shared with us her views on the power of a positive attitude based on her observations of two third-grade teachers:

> One of them is always complaining. She has difficulties with students, their parents and the administration. She talks about feeling overwhelmed by paperwork; she seems resentful about lack of recognition and extrinsic rewards. When I try to give suggestions, she is indignant and defensive. There is a lot of tension in her classroom—displays of temper, power struggles and a general lack of enthusiasm. Her kids are not well prepared when they pass on to the fourth grade.

> The other teacher, in contrast, always has a positive greeting for students, colleagues and staff. She likes to try new strategies, and she shares her enthusiasm about her lessons and results with other teachers and with me. She models a positive attitude in the classroom, and the atmosphere there is very calm. When it does get noisy, instead of tempers flaring there seems to be a lot of excited problem solving going on. I frequently hear positive comments about her from parents, and requests to put their children in her class.

> The differences between these two teachers were sharply brought out last year when we lost our reading specialist due to budget cuts. Instead of lower-achieving students

being pulled out of class for a remedial program, they now have to be taught by classroom teachers along with the rest of the students. When I made the announcement in a faculty meeting, "Teacher A" responded by blaming the system for its convoluted priorities. She returned to her classroom exasperated and disgusted. Subsequently she had her remedial students sit through the regularly scheduled activities without making much of an attempt to modify her lessons to meet their needs. She took on an attitude of "If they don't learn, don't blame me—there's nothing I can do for them." She resents having them in class. When she has to explain their poor grades to parents, she blames the administration. I can't fire her because she has tenure, but she seems so frustrated and unfulfilled in her job that I'm hoping she'll quit.

Despite the effort it took, she was clearly satisfied and enjoying her job.

"Teacher B," on the other hand, accepted the change as a challenge. She implemented whole language and cooperative group strategies supported with small-group phonics instruction for those who need it. She sought out parent volunteers and cross-grade tutors. Despite the effort it took, she was clearly satisfied and enjoying her job. She turned the problem into a "win-win" situation, and it paid off. She did everything she could to create opportunities for her students' success, and they responded by succeeding.

"Accentuate the Positive": Strategies and Techniques

That's the choice you have. You can look at your situation in a negative light and accept the consequences of this negativity—dissatisfaction, frustration, increased stress. Or, you can recognize that the price you pay for negativity is too great and put in the effort to be positive. High-performing teachers express this choice in observations such as these:

"My attitude is very different now that it was years ago. This positive approach that I have to teaching did not develop until I really started to look at what my opportunities were. I could very easily have been negative all the time. But I realized that I had the power to change this. If you look at the positive side, it allows you to build rapport with kids. It's not hard to do."

"I've been negative. I know what negativity can do. It pulls you down. It makes you sluggish. You can't produce. I have to stay positive because that gives me the power to positively impact my students. I can't buy into the negativity of the past. I won't buy into it. I'm done with that."

Let's be frank: It's easy to be negative. Once you have chosen the positive approach, you need make a diligent effort to maintain it until it becomes a habit. The good news is that there are strategies you can adopt that will help you do this.

First of all, surround yourself with positive teachers. Nothing can bring you down faster than negative, pessimistic colleagues. This is something you need to be constantly aware of. You may even choose to take the extreme step of avoiding the faculty lounge. A half hour of listening to other teachers talk about how terrible things are can send you back to the classroom with a ruling in favor of your negative lawyer.

Surround yourself with positive teachers.

Instead, choose to spend your out-of-class time with colleagues who listen to their positive lawyer. Form support networks with other positive teachers. When you make this choice, you find yourself remaining motivated to help your students. You enjoy your job more. You go home at the end of each day feeling satisfied about your mission.

There are some days, however, when negative thoughts creep in, when it's hard to stay focused on the positive aspects of your teaching situation. When this happens, you can regain your positive focus by asking yourself four questions:

1. What am I going to enjoy about today?

2. Which students am I going to help today?

3. What are the strengths of my students?

4. What am I good at?

These questions may sound superficial, but they are profoundly effective. When you're on your way to work and ruminating about

Make an effort to think about things you can look forward to.

negative aspects of your job, asking yourself what you're going to enjoy that day helps you focus on the positive. Make an effort to think about things you can look forward to. How can you make it a great day for yourself and your students? If you decide that it's going to be a great day, it's *going* to be a great day. You'll arrive at work feeling positive. The energy you create will last you throughout the day.

Instead of looking at each day in terms of the problems it might bring, consider it as an opportunity to help your students. Ask yourself which students will receive your special attention today. It's an exciting, motivating approach. Focus on specific students and decide what you're going to do to help them.

For some students your focus may be as simple as letting them know with a smile and a pleasant word that you're happy to have them in your class. For others you may choose to make a special effort. Perhaps today is the day you give Lawrence the help he needs with his penmanship. Perhaps you'll take time to have a special talk with Miriam to raise her self-confidence or give Lucas some classroom responsibility that might help him control his behavior problem. "I had a very touching moment just before Thanksgiving," one teacher told me:

> There's this little boy named Russ who came into my class
> very angry and hostile. His parents were going through

a divorce, and the negativity at home was causing him to do a lot of acting out. I try to maintain a positive, trusting atmosphere and to single out each student for special attention on a regular basis. That day it was Russ's turn. I was helping him with a report he was writing about snakes, and he looked up at me and asked me whether I had any children. I told him I didn't, but that I thought I might some day. "Well, they'd be lucky," Russ said, "'cause you'd probably be nice to them." I smiled at him and tousled his hair and told him how glad I was to have him in my class.

Remember also that the same students who present problems also have strengths. The boy who always disrupts your class may have great wit. The girl who seems so awkward at verbal expression may draw beautiful pictures. Make a point of catching your students doing something right. Give them recognition for their effort in their work, for their behavior, or for some special quality they have. This is a key strategy for maintaining a positive focus. As one teacher explains it, "Throughout the day I'm constantly looking for things that I can tell children that I like about them, qualities that I see, the work that they do. I'm constantly giving encouragement, reinforcement, positive acknowledgments all day long."

Another teacher describes the connection between such positive recognition and her own attitudes:

> The easiest way for me to stay positive is focusing on the strengths of the kids and giving them recognition for their effort and their fine behavior. When I see a child who is acting negatively, it's like he or she's holding up a big sign that says, "I need some love. I need some attention. I haven't gotten a lot lately." So, rather than focusing on the negative, or ignoring the situation, that's when I find something positive about that child to build on and help them believe in themselves.

I find something positive about that child to build on.

One way to keep in touch with students' strengths is to jot down reminders in your plan book. You have it with you every day. Use it not only to record your lesson plans but to post positive memos such as these:

- Notice when Kathy participates in discussion. Recognize her!

- Give Jordan praise when he turns in homework.

- Tell Tracy how lovely her poem was before you start correcting her spelling.

- Rafael's really been trying this week. Take a moment to let him know you've noticed.

And while you're focusing on your students' accomplishments, don't forget your own. Far too often we dwell on what we perceive to be our shortcomings and ignore our positive attributes. Get in touch with what you're good at. Identify the strengths and qualities you have that can help you achieve your mission. Maybe you have especially good communication skills. Maybe you have a special understanding of how students learn and are able to translate it into practice. Maybe your sense of humor enables you to relate well with students.

Think about what you did yesterday that was successful and made you feel good about yourself. You made a breakthrough with Monina and her reading difficulty. That project on archaeology really seems to be focusing Lester's interests.

Jot down a list of your positive qualities and achievements.

Consider your career accomplishments as an educator—the outstanding evaluations you've received, the students you persuaded to stay in school. Whatever your accomplishments may be, take some time to focus on them and on the positive feelings they produced.

Get a pen and paper right now and jot down a list of your positive qualities and achievements. Writing such a list will be an aid to remembering your skills during those times when your negative lawyer is holding forth.

While you have that paper in front of you, try this too: Make a list of strategies you can use over the next several days to help you maintain a positive focus.

Maintaining that focus is essential if you're going to live your mission. When you're feeling positive, when you bring a positive attitude to your classroom every day, you can't help but transmit that attitude to your students. As one successful teacher puts it, "I can't imagine not being positive in the classroom, because that's how I expect my students to be. If I don't have a positive attitude, there's no way I can expect them to."

> *I can't imagine not being positive in the classroom.*

Never forget that a positive attitude isn't only about saving yourself from burnout. It's a strategy for sending your students home feeling good about themselves and about school; for helping them reach their full potential. The more positive you are, the more you're going to help each and every child succeed.

And that, after all, is what you're there for.

The Power of Support

Throughout this book I have emphasized the importance of getting back in touch with your mission as an important part of combating the stress and burnout that threatens so many teachers today. As I have pointed out, frustration is the inevitable result of not being able to work toward the goals that really matter to you.

We have taken a look at some of the steps you can take to empower yourself to live your mission and in so doing minimize burnout and stress:

- Develop positive beliefs in your ability to work successfully with students and to make a difference in their lives.

- Recognize that the choices you make have an impact on your success.

- Develop problem-solving skills that empower you to overcome challenges.

- Build positive relationships with students.

- Build positive relationships with parents.

- Maintain a positive attitude, understanding that a negative attitude impedes students' learning.

> *The high-performing teacher reaches out*
> *to friends and colleagues for emotional*
> *and professional support.*

There's something else you can do—and *must do*—if you are to effectively withstand the inevitable pressures that arise.

The Necessity of an Effective Teacher Support Group

Research has shown that the absence or presence of an effective support system is *the most important factor* in managing job burnout.

A support group is more than a circle of friends. It's more than a circle of colleagues. A support group consists of colleagues and friends who meet *specific needs*, both professional and emotional.

Teachers without a support network are at risk. When problems arise they may not have the appropriate resources at hand to turn to. Without these resources—and the answers they can provide—they are far more likely to become frustrated, stressed and burned out.

Support means more than just having a friend listen to your problems. Real support involves real skills and real answers—and a forum for ensuring that you get the support when you need it.

Research has identified six different functions that individuals need to fulfill in order to have an effective support network.

1. You need technical support.

Most of us need help from our fellow educators from time to time—help figuring out some aspect of the job that eludes us for the moment. When you need that help, it's vital that you have someone to turn to whose expertise you can trust—someone with whom you can talk out problems who will not judge or think less of you for *admitting* you need help.

This person should be someone you respect as having the same skills as you, but also someone with whom you feel completely comfortable "baring your professional soul" and asking for help. No egos here. No embarrassment, either. You need someone to whom you can admit that there may be something you just don't know!

This story from a fifth-grade teacher illustrates what technical support is all about:

> I'd been teaching for several years, but I was stumped when six non-English-speaking students were suddenly transferred into my class. I felt as though I was just *expected* to know how to successfully work with them. The truth is, I didn't know what to do, particularly when I didn't even speak their language. Fortunately I had Jo to talk to. We started teaching about the same time, but she'd had a lot of experience with ESL students. It felt good to be able to go to someone and say "I need some help" without feeling as though I were a failure. With Jo's help I was able to get some specific direction and go forward with confidence.

2. You need technical challenge.

You need someone who provides technical *support* when you need it. You also need someone who will stretch you a bit professionally—who will encourage you to seek new answers that may be beyond what's just "necessary." Technical chal-

Technical challenge is what will prompt you to grow.

lenge is what will prompt you to grow. "Karen was the new teacher next door and full of enthusiasm," a teacher told us. "There always seems to be something exciting going on in her room. "

> One day while I was putting up a bulletin board for my endangered species unit, Karen popped into my classroom and asked what activities I was going to use to integrate the unit across the curriculum. Although I'd done some thematic planning before, I hadn't considered

doing it with this unit. I'd simply pulled out my file of lessons and materials and started a replay of what I'd done for the past two years.

Karen suggested a few simple activities in math, language arts and music right there on the spot, and went back to her classroom to get two literature selections that she thought would also complement the unit. I couldn't believe how spontaneous and creative she was. At first I felt a little intimidated because these suggestions were coming from a first-year teacher. But she was so positive and genuinely helpful, I was inspired.

Needless to say, the unit was not only more motivating for my class, it was more exciting and rewarding for me. Now, Karen and I get together regularly to do thematic planning.

3. You need emotional support.

As part of your support network you need somebody you know will be by your side, right or wrong. This person needn't be a professional colleague. But he or she must be someone whom you trust and who has your best interests at heart.

The importance of emotional support is illustrated by this teacher's story:

I had a friend who always had time to listen.

My first year of teaching was tough. Much of the time I felt I was in over my head, and I wasn't sure I'd made the right career decision. Fortunately I had a friend who always had time to listen. I must have called her every night that year, which may seem odd because she wasn't able to tell me how to manage my class better. She had little to offer that would help me meet the needs of an overflowing class of forty students. And she sure didn't know much about the challenges of urban teaching. But she listened, and that meant everything. There were nights when I was ready to quit. But after our conversations I somehow had the strength to return to the classroom the next day.

4. You need emotional challenge.

Emotional challenge is far different from emotional support. Emotional challenge is also given by someone who will stand by you and who cares about you but who is not afraid to confront you when you're not doing something the way it should be done. "A couple of years ago I was having lots of trouble with one boy, Ronny, in my seventh-grade lit class," a middle-school teacher told us.

He was defiant and rude. Every day seemed worse than the day before and I complained a lot about him to just about everyone. I got lots of sympathy, too, and I guess I liked that. When I complained to Ellen, though, I got something different. She really called me on it. Deep down I knew

She more or less told me to stop complaining.

I wasn't doing everything I could to help this student, and Ellen let me know that in no uncertain terms. She more or less told me to stop complaining and do something about the situation—if not for my sake then for the sake of my student who was, after all, the one I should have been thinking of. She was blunt, but she was right. Ellen is one of my closest friends, and when she talks I listen. Instead of focusing on only me, I started looking at Ronny from a different perspective, asking myself *why* he was such a problem. Of course things didn't turn around overnight, but once I focused on problem solving instead of complaining, *I* was in control and that made all the difference in the world.

5. You need someone who is an active listener.

In your support group you need somebody who listens, who asks clarifying questions, who at times paraphrases what you're saying, and who helps you see the world a little bit more clearly by listening.

Here's what an active listener *isn't*: You're having a tough day. As soon as you get to the teachers' room at lunchtime you start sharing some of the more memorable parts of that day. You have an audience, all right. *Everyone's* listening. But you're barely finished with two or three particularly pithy vignettes when a colleague pipes in with, "You call that a bad day? Let me tell you about mine." And the conversation is off and running.

An active listener doesn't egg a conversation on or just passively listen. An active listener is a *participant* in your conversation, a participant with a very specific role to play. He or she listens with a purpose—to help you see a situation more clearly.

This story from a fourth-grade teacher tells the value of active listening:

> *An active listener is a participant in your conversation.*
>
> I was so angry one day I could hardly see straight. My principal had called me in to tell me that one of my student's parents had complained that the assignments I gave were meaningless, that his child was ignored and basically very unhappy. I was new to the school at that time and the principal didn't seem pleased at all.
>
> I was angry and embarrassed. I'm a caring teacher and do not intentionally ignore or bore my students! To have these charges leveled at me through my administrator just set me off.
>
> By the time I talked it over with Jeff I was fuming. First, he just let me let off steam. Then, when I was calmer, he asked questions. Who was this student? What could be going on that would prompt the call from his parent? Had I met the parent? What sort of relationship had I

developed with him?

Well, the student's name was Raul, and he was new to the school—new to the country, in fact. I'd only barely spoken to his father even though I had intended to call him. Through my conversation with Jeff I realized that the parent's call to the principal could be interpreted as a call for help for the child—and not necessarily a malicious slap against *me*. The fact that the parent had called the principal instead of me was something I couldn't do anything about, but I sure could take action now. Instead of directing anger at the parent I could look at things from a different perspective. Here was a parent who must care. Now what could I do to take advantage of that?

As things turned out, that was actually the start of a positive relationship with a concerned parent. I learned that the call to the principal was made because that's the way things were done in his native country. The boredom his son was claiming was in large part the result of his feelings of isolation in a new environment. The parent had acted out of *concern* for his child, and together we worked a lot of things out to help Raul adjust to his new life.

One thing stays in my mind, though. If I hadn't had Jeff to talk things out with, this story could have had a very different ending. I might have gone to class the next day resenting Raul *and* his parent. I might never have had the motivation (and insight) to reach out to them and develop a positive relationship.

6. Finally, you need somebody who shares your sense of reality.

Well-meaning friends and colleagues can offer advice, but unless they share your reality, and really understand "where you're coming from," that advice and support may not meet your needs. For example, if many of your challenges arise from being in a school that is plagued by drugs, violence and poverty, you need support from colleagues who understand exactly what that means. If your challenges stem from the frustration of inadequate facilities and materials, you need colleagues who relate to that as well. It's just common sense. We tend to give far more credence to advice from those we respect as truly understanding our situations.

An effective support network depends on friends and colleagues who can provide each of these six types of support. Knowing this, what do you do next?

Organizing a Support Group

Support groups don't just happen. You have to be part of the team that makes them. Talk to colleagues you feel would be active, positive members of such a group. Explore what a support group could do for all of you and set a plan in motion to get yours started.

> *Talk to colleagues you feel would be active, positive members.*

Support groups are different from school to school—and from teachers to teachers. They differ depending on what issues you want to tackle. One group might organize around a specific curriculum interest. Another might have a focus of a more politically activist nature. Whatever the focus, however, all successful support groups share these common themes:

There must be a high level of trust among members.

Members of the group must feel free to speak, share, ask for help and bare their feelings. A support group is no place for suspicion and judgment.

Members must commit to consistent involvement and participation.

A support group is only as strong as its members' commitment to *staying* involved. Attendance at group meetings cannot be haphazard. In a support group you rely on others and they rely on you. Meetings must be scheduled, and schedules must be adhered to.

Group members must be active listeners.

As I mentioned earlier, just listening is not adequate for problem solving. Group members must ask clarifying questions and help others arrive at meaningful conclusions. Be sure your support group members can all fulfill this important role.

Everything that goes on must be confidential.

You need your support group to be a forum for venting frustration, sharing disappointments, asking questions, trying out solutions and taking risks—no matter how far-fetched they may seem. You need to know that what goes on in your group stays in your group. Confidentiality is a must.

Finally, and most important perhaps, fill your support group with people who are positive and proactive. There's no room for negativity in a well-functioning support group. You want energy and good feelings. Make sure you have it, and make sure that others do too.

The Power of Planning

In this book you have learned several techniques that can empower you to fulfill your mission. There is, however, one last attribute you must acquire if you're going to integrate these strategies into a program for maximizing your effectiveness. You need to be able to *plan*— to organize and prioritize your time.

As a teacher you have incredible demands on your time. There are papers to grade, staff meetings to attend, lessons to design. As you've read the last few chapters, it's likely that this issue has come up again and again. You've probably asked yourself, "But where am I going to find the *time* to reach out to each student on a one-to-one basis? How do I phone parents, write positive notes, find creative strategies for meeting my challenges, attend school activities and still have time to teach the curriculum?"

It's a valid question, and the answer we learn from high-performing teachers is this: You need to prioritize your time. You need to take proactive steps to *focus your efforts* if you're going to achieve the best possible results.

There's a story that illustrates the concept. Two woodsmen got up one morning and sawed trees until dark. The first woodsman worked without stopping. The second woodsman took a ten-minute break every hour. At the end of the day, the second woodsman had cut a dozen more trees than the first.

The first woodsman said, "How could you have cut more trees than I? You were taking breaks all the time, while I was going nonstop, sawing, sawing, sawing." The second woodsman looked at him and replied, "During those breaks I was sharpening my saw."

And that in essence is what you must do. You will never get the best possible results simply by sawing, sawing, sawing. To reach your full potential as a teacher, to truly make a difference in the classroom, you need to keep your saw sharp. You need to know how you can most effectively allocate your time.

> *The high-performing teacher achieves maximum results by planning the best use of his or her time.*

Focus on What's Important, Not on What's Urgent

One useful way to organize and prioritize the demands on your time is to divide all your activities into four categories, depending on their *urgency* and *importance*.*

Please note that *urgent* and *important* do not mean the same thing. An activity that is urgent is one that requires your immediate attention. An activity that is important is one that is *critical to your desired results*. Too often you're called upon to deal with urgencies, leaving you little time to devote to what's important. As you read the next few paragraphs, take a few moments and think about the different activities that take up your work time. Consider whether each activity is urgent, important, both or neither. Then jot them down in the appropriate column in the graph on page 128.

*Adapted from Stephen R. Covey, *The Seven Habits of Highly Effective People*. New York: Simon and Schuster, 1989

Category 1: Urgent and Important

Category 1 is where you assign activities that are both urgent and important—for example, teaching the core curriculum, addressing academic and behavior problems, or dealing with angry parents. These are activities to which you must give your immediate attention, or your efforts will quickly come to a standstill.

Category 3: Urgent, but Unimportant

Let's skip over Category 2 for now; we'll get back to it in a moment. Category 3 is where you place activities that require your immediate attention but have little or no bearing on your mission. Examples include most paperwork, assemblies and staff meetings. They're bureaucratic necessities, but you could ignore them without any negative impact on your overall effectiveness.

Category 4: Not Urgent, not Importnat

In Category 4 are activities that are neither urgent nor important, for example, decorating your classroom. You can generally recognize these activities as low-priority items.

Take a few moments and think about the items you wrote down in Categories 3 and 4. Jot down some notes on how you might realistically reduce the time you spend on these activities. Which ones could be eliminated or made more efficient? Which ones could be delegated to students, aides, or parent volunteers?

Category 2: Not Urgent, Critically Important

Now let's go back to Category 2. Here is where you assign most of the activities that I've emphasized in this book—activities that may not require your immediate attention but that are *critically important* to the fulfillment of your mission:

- reaching out to students
- taking proactive steps to prevent problems from arising
- building students' self-esteem

Category 1 URGENT AND IMPORTANT	Category 2 NOT URGENT, CRITICALLY IMPORTANT	Category 3 URGENT, BUT UNIMPORTANT	Category 4 NOT URGENT, NOT IMPORTANT
Example: Dealing with behavior problems	Example: Establishing positive relationships with students	Example: Paperwork	Example: Decorating classroom

- building relationships with parents

- taking care of your own needs

- seeking new solutions to persistent problems

Category 2 is where you must focus your planning efforts. It's crucial to make plans to spend some medium- and long-range time on them if you're going to be effective in the classroom. Category 2 is where you get your daily satisfaction and sense

It's crucial to make plans if you're going to be effective in the classroom.

of accomplishment. Category 2 is ultimately where you fulfill your mission.

Category 2 is where you sharpen your saw.

"You can't shoot from the hip," is how one teacher expresses it:

> Each class period comes and goes so fast. Your mind is on the lesson, your students' behavior, and there are un-expected things that come up. Yet there are those other things you've got to do, like building relationships with students. Unless you consciously plan to integrate them into your day, take the time to write them down and commit to doing them as part of the lesson, they may go undone. And then you're sunk. It's like not taking care of your car—you put off getting your oil changed, and now your engine's conked out, you're stranded, and you have a lot of expensive repairs to make.

"Time is money," wise old Ben Franklin said. Consider your planning as an investment in time with a guaranteed high yield. The more time you invest in planning your activities in Category 2, the less you'll need to spend on the urgencies of Category 1. No, you don't *need* to establish a relationship with each student right now, but if you do, you may prevent a crisis from developing down the road. You don't *need* to contact parents right now, but if you do, you may avoid a negative relationship with them three months from now. You don't *need* to establish a support group this week, but if you start seeking out positive teachers now you'll be that much more likely to resist negative thoughts later.

"I learned about planning from a principal I worked for," one teacher tells us:

> He had a sign posted in his office that said, "Fail to plan, plan to fail." At the first staff meeting of the year he always used to talk about planning things in writing as the key
>
> *He had a sign posted that said, "Fail to plan, plan to fail."*
>
> to preventing problems from developing. The teachers who were new to the school would roll their eyes, but after trying it for a year they'd be sold. Taking a few minutes each day for planning really saves time in the long run. You create a plan for preventive action, and you commit yourself to acting on it. When a problem does pop up, you've got a plan in place that enables you to handle it without a lot of stress.

Planning Your Time

You didn't go into teaching to deal with behavior problems, angry parents, and burnout. You became a teacher because you wanted to make a difference in students' lives. If you take the time to keep your saw sharp, you'll have better results than the teacher who just keeps hacking away. If you make a point of planning time for your truly important activities even though they may not be urgent, you'll find that it pays off every day of the year. Your students will show incredible results, and you'll go home at the end of each day feeling satisfied and motivated.

You can do it by spending just ten minutes at the end of the day planning your Category 2 activities. The first step is to sit down and ask yourself these questions:

- How am I going to build relationships with students?

- How am I going to prevent problems from occurring?

- What can I do to build my students' self-esteem?

- What am I going to do to reach out to parents?

- What will be the result of this planning?

Let's take a look at how you can address each of these questions.

How am I going to build relationships with students?

"When I started teaching my worst fear was that the kids wouldn't like me or be open with me," an award-winning teacher recalls:

> I had done my student teaching with a really hot seventh-grade teacher who had an amazing rapport with his students. The day before I started doing it for real I sat down and asked myself just what it was he did to develop such terrific relationships. One thing I'd noticed about him was the notes he wrote to himself in his daily planner. Every day there were specific reminders to give special attention to two or three students, so that over several weeks everyone in the class would get stroked. I started doing this myself the first week of school. Sometimes I'd write a reminder in my plan book, other times it was a quick note on a Post-It™ or in the margin of a newspaper while I was driving to work. I was able to achieve wonderful results in getting students to respond to me, and I've used the same strategy ever since.

Every day there were reminders to give special attention to two or three students.

Scan your class list at the end of each day to determine which students would most benefit from some individual attention tomorrow. Would Kerri appreciate a positive note home? Would a few words in the morning be special to Wayne? Maybe your relationship with Robin would benefit from an after-school call.

Focus on students who are having problems and ask yourself, "Okay, what can I do to make trust deposits tomorrow?" Maybe Joe would appreciate a brief talk, a little concern about what's going on in his home life. Maybe you'll want to ask Kim how her piano recital went on Saturday. Maybe with Alicia all that's needed is a positive comment about her math homework.

Write down what you're going to do.

Take your focus one step further—*write down* what you're going to do, either in your plan book or in some specially designated place. Writing it down will help you commit to actually doing it, and it will help you develop the habit of planning your relationship-building in a systematic way.

How am I going to prevent problems from occurring?

No teacher is so naive that he or she doesn't expect problems to occur. The trouble is that most teachers simply react to problems when they arise instead of taking steps to head them off. By failing to take care of Category 2 necessities, they allow them to escalate into Category 1 urgencies.

High-performing teachers take proactive steps to prevent problems from occurring. They take time to assess what is working and what isn't. They take preventive action now instead of corrective action later. "When my school instituted cooperative-group learning, I could tell right away that I was doing something wrong," a third-grade teacher relates:

> My kids weren't successful working in groups. Instead of the quiet hum of busy children at work, my room seemed chaotic and noisy. It was frustrating for me and disorienting for the kids. They were floundering, and behavior problems were rampant. But cooperative learning was what the district had mandated that year, and I was stuck with it.
>
> It was all very discouraging until I attended an inservice where we learned strategies for organizing the groups,

structuring tasks, smoothing out procedures. I realized that all I'd really been planning was lesson content. I'd been trying to improvise on that content, like a jazz player with a lead sheet, and what I needed was a note-by-note score. The next time I planned a group activity, I mapped out on a separate sheet of paper how I was going to organize and structure it. I stapled it to my plan book and used it as a guide. The result was a much more appropriate and productive atmosphere, and the amazing thing was that the planning took only ten minutes of my time.

Preventive problem-solving is like preventive medicine. The time to stop smoking and start your exercise program is *before* you develop heart trouble. What issues in your classroom might benefit from some judicious planning? Academics? If your lessons aren't working, maybe you'd better experiment with new teaching strategies before things get out of hand. Behavior management? Maybe this is the time to institute a whole-class positive recognition reward system. Don't wait until things go wrong—take a few minutes to assess what *could* go wrong. Then plan what you're going to do to keep things right.

Plan what you're going to do to keep things right.

What can I do to build my students' self-esteem?

For most teachers building students' self-esteem is a vital part of their mission. You can best guide students toward success if you take the time to build individual self-worth enhancements into your activities.

"There was a boy in my fifth-grade class whose sense of competence was wearing thin," a Seattle-area teacher tells us:

> Wes had received failing grades from teachers in the past. He was constantly being compared with an older brother who was a football star at the local high school. He was often put down by peers on the playground and on the bus. I made a point of creating opportunities for Wes to

feel competent. I broke down activities into achievable increments and made sure that I praised him for each success. I stayed away from extrinsic rewards because I wanted his reinforcement to come from within—from looking at himself and feeling proud. I kept a folder of his work and showed it to him from time to time so that he could see the progress he had made. Most important, I took every opportunity to let him know that I liked and accepted him just the way he was.

Consider the needs of your students during your planning sessions.

Consider the needs of your students during your daily planning sessions. You may want to structure a lesson in a way that will help Michelle develop a positive attitude about herself. You may have an idea for an activity to help Kevin learn self-management skills and personal responsibility, or to help Jenny establish positive peer relationships. It all comes down to planning what you are going to do each day to be the best teacher you can be.

What am I going to do to reach out to parents?

This is an area that absolutely requires advance planning. You can't just pick up a phone and call parents. You need to take time to plan when you are going to call and what you are going to say. Since you're already planning your parent-outreach efforts to that extent, it's only a small step to commit to making it a daily priority.

Go through your plan book and identify two or three students who would benefit from a closer relationship between you and their parents. Designate those parents for positive notes this week. Is there a special activity coming up that parents might like to hear about? Use your daily planning time to draft a letter for the class to send home. Is there a student who might benefit from a positive phone call to his or her parents? Jot a reminder to yourself to make that call. Is there a problem developing that you want to head off? Write a memo to yourself to call a parent. Is there a mom or dad who has given you a lot of support lately? Remind yourself to pick up the phone to express your appreciation.

"I'd never had any luck getting parents to come to back-to-school night," recalls one teacher who has since learned to appreciate the power of planning:

> I'd send out invitations and reminders through the kids, but I'd never get more than ten or eleven parents out of a possible fifty. A few years ago I was brooding about this in my classroom just before I went home for the day. Back-to-school night was the following evening. I'd prepared a nice presentation, and I was a little let down about the prospect of doing my act before an empty house. Then I hit on the idea of phoning a few parents to boost attendance a little. I took my plan book home and started calling the parents with whom I'd had contact that year. I got mostly answering machines, but the parents I did reach sounded positive enough that I ended up calling all my kids' parents and reminding them to come.
>
> The personal touch worked like a charm. I got better than fifty percent attendance. The next year I made the calls a few days in advance and had almost a full house. The experience taught me how useful and how necessary it is to plan ahead if I want to engage parents.

The experience taught me how necessary it is to plan ahead.

What will be the result of this planning?

Planning the proactive use of your time can help you build positive relationships with students, prevent problems from developing, build student self-esteem and secure parents' support. The last thing you need to consider during your daily planning is how to build a better relationship with *you*—how to use your time to safeguard your emotional health as it relates to your job.

How are you going to stay renewed? How are you going to stay fired up? Are you going to organize a support group? It won't happen unless you plan it. How are you going to find the answers to challenges you face? You need to plan where you're going to look for them.

This planning time is what will empower you to make a difference. The high-performing teacher spends ten minutes each day planning how to live his or her mission in the classroom—and that teacher is no different from you or me. None of the high-performing teachers quoted in this book is any more gifted, any more "natural" at teaching than you are. They are making a difference in the classroom simply because they have made choices that have put them in control of their efforts.

"Why do I feel that I can make a difference?" one such teacher reflects:

> It goes back to the word "I." I have choices in life. I can look at them and say, "This is something that's fighting me, something I can't deal with," and I can shut down. Or I can choose to say, "How am I going to deal with this? How am I going to overcome this?"
>
> Because the bottom line is, we're not dealing with a product like an automobile or an article of clothing. We're dealing with a human being, and we can't just write them off. We can't write them off.

These choices can be yours too. You have learned the strategies by which high-performing teachers reach deep within themselves and

Ignite the power that lies within us all.

ignite the power that lies within us all. You've always had it in you to be a high-performing teacher—to make a difference in your students' lives. Now you have the tools you need to do it—to determine what you can and cannot control, to rise above the challenges, to motivate yourself and your students, to be the best possible teacher you can be. It's simply a matter of making choices, of changing habits.

Now go on out there and live your mission!

Bibliography

Ailes, R. *You Are the Message: Secrets of the Master Communicators*. Homewood, Illinois: Dow Jones Irwin Press, 1988.

Allinder, R. "I Think I Can, I Think I Can: The Effect of Self-Efficacy on Teacher Effectiveness," *Beyond Behavior*, Vol. 4, No. 2, p. 29, Winter 1993.

Barth, R. *Improving Schools from Within*. San Francisco, California: Jossey-Bass, Inc. Publishers, 1990.

Bedley, G. *The Big R: Responsibility*. Irvine, California: Peoplewide Publishers, 1985.

Borba, M. *Esteem Builders*. Rolling Hills Estates, California: Del Mar Press, 1989.

Burns, D. *The Feeling Good Handbook: Using the New Mood Therapy in Everyday Life*. New York, New York: William Morrow Company, 1989.

California Task Force to Promote Self-esteem and Personal and Social Responsibility. *Towards A State of Esteem*. Sacramento, California: California State Department of Education, 1990.

Call, J. Jr. "The Case of the Vanishing Teachers," *Phi Delta Kappan*, 66, p. 224, 1984.

Campbell, L. "How to Improve Teacher Morale and School Effectiveness," *NASSP Tips for Principals*, pp. 3-4, November 1990.

Canfield, J., and Siccone, F. *101 Ways to Develop Student Self-esteem and Responsibility*, Vol. 1. Boston, Massachusetts: Allyn and Bacon, 1993.

Connolly, C., and Sander, W. "Teacher Stress—An Ongoing Problem that Needs Attention." Paper presented at the Annual Meeting of the Association of Teacher Educators, Atlanta, GA: 1986.

Coopersmith, S. R. *Developing Motivation in Young Children*. San Francisco, California: Albion, 1975.

Covey, S. *The Seven Habits of Highly Effective People*. New York, New York: Simon and Schuster, 1989.

Covington, M. "Recent Research Findings On Self-Esteem." Paper presented at the Annual California State Conference on Self-Esteem. San Jose, California: 1988.

Csikszentmihaly, M., and McCormack, J. "The Influence of Teachers," *Phi Delta Kappan*, pp. 415-419, February 1986.

Curtis, J., and Altman, H. "The Relationship Between Teacher Self-Concept and the Self-Concept of Students," *Child Study Journal*, No. 7, 1977.

Dembo, M., and Gibson, S., "Teacher's Sense of Efficacy: An Important Factor in School Improvement," *The Elementary School Journal*, Vol. 86, No. 2, pp. 173-184, November 1985.

Emmer, E., and Hickman, J. "Teacher Efficacy in Classroom Management and Discipline," *Educational & Psychological Measurement*, Vol. 51, pp. 755-765, 1991.

Fielding, M. *Personality and Situational Correlates of Teacher Stress and Burnout*, Unpublished study in the library of the University of Oregon, 1982.

Fox, C., and Metzger, M. "Friendly Persuasion," *Teacher Magazine*, Vol. 2, No. 7, pp. 33-37, April 1991.

Friedland, S., "Building Student Self-Esteem for School Improvement," *National Association of Secondary School Principals*, Vol. 76, pp. 96-103, January 1992.

Gibbs, J. *Tribes: A Process for Social Development and Cooperative Learning*. Santa Rosa, California: Center Source Publications, 1987.

Gold, Y., and Michael, W. "Academic Self-Concept Correlates of Potential Burnout in a Sample of First Semester Elementary Practice Teachers: A Concurrent Validity Study," *Educational and Psychological Measurement*, 45, 909-914, 1985.

Gordon, T. *Teaching Children Self-Discipline at Home and School: New Ways for Parents and Teachers to Build Self-Control, Self-Esteem and Self-Reliance*. New York, New York: Times Books, 1989.

Greenwood, G., Olejnik, S. and Parkay, F. "Relationships Between Four Teacher Efficacy Belief Patterns and Selected Teacher Characteristics," *Journal of Research and Development in Education*, Vol. 23, No. 2, pp. 102-106, Winter 1990.

Grossnickly, D., and Stephens, R. *Developing Personal and Social Responsibility*. Malibu, California: Pepperdine University Press, National School Safety Center, 1992.

Holly, W. "Student Self-esteem and Academic Success," *Oregon School Study Council*, Eugene, Oregon: Vol. 31 (2), 1987.

Huston, J. "Teacher Burnout and Effectiveness" *Education*, Vol. 110, pp. 70-78, Fall 1989.

Jersild, A. *When Teachers Face Themselves*. New York, New York: Teachers College Press, 1985.

John-Roger and McWilliam, P. *You Can't Afford the Luxury of a Negative Thought*. Santa Monica, California: Prelude Press, 1991.

Johnson, D., and Johnson, R. *Teaching Students to Be Peacemakers*. Edina, Minnesota: Interaction Book Company, 1991.

Juhasz, A. "Teacher Self-Esteem, a Triple Roll Approach to this Forgotten Dimension," *Education*, Vol. 111, pp. 234-241, Winter 1990.

Kostelnik, M., Stein, L., and Hickman, J. "Children's Self-esteem—The Verbal Environment," *Childhood Education*, Vol. 65, pp. 29-32, Fall 1988.

Kreidler, W. *Creative Conflict Resolution: More Than 200 Activities for Keeping Peace in the Classroom*. Glenview, Illinois: Scott, Foresman and Company, 1984.

Lerner, B. *Self-Esteem and Excellence: The Choice and the Paradox*. American Educator Winner, pp. 10-16, 1985.

Maeroff, G. *Voices From The Classroom: Exceptional Teachers Speak*. Washington, D.C.: National Foundation for the Improvement of Education, 1990. Marston, S. *The Magic of Encouragement: Nurturing Your Child's Self-Esteem*. New York, New York: William Morrow, 1990.

Maslow, A. *Towards a Psychology of Being* (Second Edition). New York, New York: Vannostrand, 1968.

McIntyre, T. "The Relationship Between Locus of Control and Teacher Burnout," *British Journal of Psychology*, 54(2), pp. 234-238, 1984.

Merrill, A. *Connections: Quadrant II Time Management*. Salt Lake City, Utah: Institute for Principle-Centered Leadership, 1989.